Victory

and

The Lord's Healing Touch

Published 1900

by Kathryn Kuhlman

Victory in Jesus

Kathryn Kuhlman

Foreword

The Holy Spirit, Jesus' gift to His church, is changeless; and God's purposes are never disappointed or defeated. Kathryn Kuhlman's earthly ministry ceased with her death in 1976 ; but countless lives are still being touched for God through her books and the many radio tapes that she prepared in her lifetime.

Again and again she acknowledged her nothingness and that every miracle that took place in her meetings — from the healing of physical bodies to those who found Christ as Savior — was a direct result of the power of God.

For many years her inspired and down-to-earth heart-to-heart talks over nearly one hundred radio stations proved to be a rich fountain-head of nourishing spiritual food relating to everyday living. The might and life-changing power of these messages has not diminished with the passing of time.

After carefully reviewing her taped subject matter, this series titled "Victory in Jesus," was chosen for print. In addition, we have included an earlier publication, "The Lord's Healing Touch."

It is our intent to bring to you, the reader, the impact of Kathryn Kuhlman's anointed words. Thus we pray that the following chapters shall be a source of blessing, Holy Ghost inspiration and a challenge to encourage you to a new and higher level of the victorious Christian life.

Marguerite Hartner

The Kathryn Kuhlman Foundation

Kathryn Kuhlman

Table of Content

Victory In Jesus

-By Kathryn Kuhlman

Prayers God Hears	1
Now is the Time	10
Day By Day	15
Confident Rest	24
Temptations	31
Snares and Pitfalls	36
Other Dangers	47
God, Our Provider	55
Holiness	61
Mere Religion	71
Feelings	78
With Your Eyes on Jesus	86
Let It Shine	90
The Secret	96

The Lord's Healing Touch
-By Kathryn Kuhlman

Faith !	103
Your Faith	105
A Reasonable Doctrine	110
Miracles of Healing	120
The Healing Virtue	123
How To Touch the Lord	129
The Prayer of Faith	132
Foundation of Faith	135
The Bible Prescription	139
Anointing With Oil	141
The Healing Testimony	143
Conclusion	147

Kathryn Kuhlman

Prayers God Hears

I feel compelled to touch lightly on the subject of prayer before I begin this series on how to live victoriously; but first may I share with you a letter I received from Northridge, California.

For the first time last night, I accidentally turned on your television program and I was so emotionally glued to every word you said that I thought and thought about the program and your comments all day long.

"I had heard of you several years ago when a friend purchased your book, I BELIEVE IN MIRACLES, and since that time I had forgotten your name. But last night it was quite an experience for me to see you and your guests. I was deeply touched by the lady who went through such turmoil with the little son who had the club foot. In fact, as I already stated, I thought about it all day long.

"It seems I have had just one thing after another in my own life: illness, financial troubles, family problems, etc.

Yes, I'm a firm believer in prayer, but I have prayed so long. I have prayed so hard for many things that seem to never come true, and I so often wonder if God hears me.

"I'm writing to you, Miss Kuhlman, to explain to me just what you meant by praying to God. The lady on your telecast said that she realized that she had been praying wrong. This is the part I didn't understand. She went on to say that the day her son walked, she was talking to God and didn't realize that her son had walked across the floor. Now I'm wondering if I am praying wrong. Would you please. Miss Kuhlman, take a minute and tell me how to pray?

"Thank you so much for a most inspirational half - hour. I will look forward to it every Sunday evening." and the woman signed her full name and gave her address.

The other day during one of our radio broadcasts, a man and his wife were talking. His wife had received a wonderful healing, a real miracle. The gentleman himself was telling of a physical healing he had received, and then he turned to me and said something I shall never forget. His eyes were brimming with tears as he spoke, "But the greatest thing of it all, greater than any physical healing, was the fact that you taught me how to pray!"

As long as I live, I shall remember that man's words, and remember the look on his face when he made the statement — "But the greatest thing of all, you taught me how to pray!

Consider something. Prayer is the greatest power God has given to you and me. There is no greater power that God has given to any human being than the power of prayer; but there can be no real praying and you cannot know how to pray until first of all you realize that wonderful relationship that you have with God the Father, Jesus Christ the Son, and the Holy Spirit.

Prayer is much more than "saying" prayers. You would be amazed how many people write to me and say, "Will you please send me that prayer that you prayed?" Prayer is something that comes from deep on the inside of one. Nothing has been written out. Nothing has been memorized. That is not real praying to say something that someone else has written. In a very simple way, even while I am talking to someone, I may close my eyes, and often with my eyes open I begin to pray. A printed prayer can sometimes help you become God conscious or create an attitude of prayer, but that is not really praying.

In order to make this as simple as I possibly can, you must realize that prayer involves a relationship with God. The fact that God is our creator is one thing that all human beings have in common. Not everyone, however, has taken advantage of that glorious relationship when God becomes more than creator — that moment when He becomes one's Heavenly Father. This relationship must begin by accepting Jesus Christ, the divine Son of God, as Personal Savior.

Therefore, not everyone can come into His presence and say, "Father, my Heavenly Father," because God does not become one's Heavenly Father and there cannot be that relationship except there be that born again spiritual experience first, accepting Jesus Christ as Savior Once you have had that spiritual experience, accepting Jesus Christ and what He did for you on the cross, reaching out and accepting Christ as Savior by faith, you can be sure that you are now God's child. It's not complicated at all. Simply look up and say, "Wonderful Jesus, I accept for myself that which You did for me on the cross and because God's Word promises that ''him that Cometh unto me I will in no wise cast out" (John 6:37), the transaction is done — it's complete. From that instant, you can have that wonderful relationship where God, your creator, is your Heavenly Father.

I'm sure you would not say that you found it difficult to come into the presence of your earthly parent and converse with your father or mother. I shall never forget my relationship with my Papa. If you know me well, you are aware that of all the human beings that I have known, my relationship with Papa was the greatest. When I was a child, I would hang on him, I would love him ! Mama would say to me, "Stop hanging on Papa !" He was still carrying me when my legs were so long they would drag on the pavement. He would no sooner get home each evening, put his coat in the closet, before I was hanging on him. He had no chance to wash his hands or comb his hair. He would sit down to rest a minute and I was on his lap, my arms around his neck, chattering, my words coming so fast. Mama would try again, "Kathryn, Papa is tired. Just sit down and be quiet."

But I couldn't! There was so much to talk about, so much had happened and I had to tell Papa everything. Papa had to know. I knew that Papa wanted to know. There wasn't a thing that happened that day that I didn't tell Papa. There never was a person that was easier to converse with than Papa. It was so natural. When something happened, instinctively I would think, "I must tell Papa."

Perhaps that is why my relationship with the Heavenly Father is real and very personal. I never memorized anything to tell Papa. It came spontaneously, and that's the way it is with my

Heavenly Father.

There must be the knowledge of that relationship between yourself and your Heavenly Father, and when you talk to Him, you must be conscious of His power. He is all-powerful, and not only that. He is concerned about every detail in that life of yours. I wish I had the vocabulary and the ability to help you understand that He is interested in you as an individual. Your needs, your troubles, your heartbreaks are His concern. When those tears roll down your cheeks. He sees those falling tears and He is interested. In the midnight hour when you feel there isn't a soul who cares, the family is asleep and you feel so all alone ; you can hear the breathing of the one next to you or you can hear the restlessness of the child in the next room : remember, God is there, closer to you than the next beat of your heart.

You may be a mother whose son is in the military service thousands of miles away. In your home in that midnight hour, you may be praying a prayer for his protection. God will not only hear that prayer that you are praying, but He is concerned about that boy of yours and He will put a wall of fire around that son. He will give His angels charge over that boy. He will not mock the desire of your heart. He will not turn a deafened ear to the cry of your soul, I promise you. He loves you. He is concerned about you, your loved ones and your needs.

You who are so steeped in sin can know victory and a new life although you have tried everything under God's heaven to bring about your deliverance. There is a God who is concerned and He is waiting for you to come into His presence through Jesus Christ His only begotten Son, to pray that prayer of confession. He will set you free if you really want to be set free, and you really want deliverance. When we come before the Father's Throne, we have a great Mediator, we have a High Priest, Jesus Christ.

Before Jesus went back to heaven, He made one thing very clear : that He was leaving us His Name to use (John 16:23, 24). All that we have to do is present His Name before the throne of God and we have a hearing. We know that God sees us as perfect and righteous and holy through the person of His Son. He also hears our prayer when we come in the Name of Jesus. Any man, any woman who will come before the throne of God and into His presence through the person of His only begotten Son, Jesus, will have a hearing.

Finally, there is the Holy Spirit, the mighty power of the Trinity, who is here on this earth to do the Father's bidding, to do what Jesus would do were He here in person (John 16:13, 14). In that moment when we come in the Name of Jesus before the Father's throne, God hears us and He gives the nod to the Holy Spirit who does the work and brings to pass the answer to our prayers.

With every atom of my being, I pray that the Holy Spirit will have taught you the simplicity of prayer, and that He has made the presence and power of Jesus a reality to your soul.

Now is the Time

This series of messages on living victoriously can be very profitable to you, for it is a matter vitally important to ALL who are Christians ; and what I have to say is surely good old-fashioned Missouri cornbread. It is not stiff nor fancy, but good for you. Try to forget that it is Kathryn Kuhlman who is having this little heart-to-heart talk with you. Keep your mind and your heart open to the Lord Jesus Christ and His Holy Spirit. Never forget this very simple fact, one that is often overlooked : the only time that we can live a Christian life is NOW. Right now! If you forget everything else that I may say to you, remember this simple but vitally important fact. NOW we are alive. NOW is the time for opportunities. NOW is that challenging moment. It is easy to procrastinate and put off until tomorrow or next week what we should do today. We can look ahead to that time when life is almost over and think that is when we will prepare to meet God and make provision for Eternity. My friend, it is NOW!

In the riches of divine grace, our Heavenly Father has made a wonderful provision for constant, consistent and unbroken victory on the part of everyone of His children, a victory that is unaffected by circumstances, however depressing or extreme they may be. This gift of God's grace in large measure is unaccepted however : partly because of ignorance as to its nature and value, and also on the ground of its terms, for its terms require a surrender which the average Christian is unwilling to make.

Things gotten cheaply are usually 'cheap,' you know. The things that are costly are usually the treasures that are most valuable and which we appreciate most. One of the most extraordinary things about the victorious life is that although it is clearly taught in the scriptures, it is frequently unrecognized by Bible students. That is something that has been very difficult for me to understand. And why is it that so many men in our pulpits today, so many of our seminary students, so many of our spiritual leaders have not recognized this wonderful life of unbroken victory with the Lord Jesus Christ? You may have a thorough knowledge of the Bible yet know nothing of this truth experimentally. And the fact still remains that you cannot give to someone else more than you have experienced yourself. If only you can catch the glory of the truth that I am trying to give to you regarding the victorious life, then you will possess a measure of God's grace that will revolutionize and change your entire spiritual life. It has been one of the greatest truths that it has been my privilege to receive from the Master.

Perhaps you are saying, "But you do not understand my circumstances. If you only knew the trials that I face, if you had to live with my husband, if you had a son and daughter like my son and daughter, if you had to put up with neighbors like my neighbors, if you had to work where I work . . . then you would not be able to say there is a place in the Lord Jesus Christ where you can have constant victory and be happy."

I understand more perfectly than you think, my friend. But, I am not looking to that godless husband of yours, or to those trying teen-agers at your house, or those neighbors of yours, or the folk with whom you have to work. I am still looking to Jesus, and we have His promise which guarantees that we can be not only conquerors but MORE than conquerors over all these things, over all circumstances, over every difficulty (Romans 8:37). Not through our own efforts are we more than conqueror; but through Him, through the Lord Jesus Christ. To me that is thrilling and wonderful.

I am convinced that some folk really do not know how to live a daily consistent, victorious Christian life. Remember something: as Christian believers, we are not only living a spiritual life, but there is the physical aspect of life, too. No one can deny that this spiritual life is marvelous ; but remember, after you have been born again and after you have had that wonderful experience of having been filled with the Holy Spirit, you must never lose sight of the fact that you are still in a body of flesh, in an old material world. Your neighbors have not changed, the folk with whom you work have not changed, and the enemy of your soul has not been converted. You find that you still have to work for a living, you have to eat, you have to sleep, you have the same husband or you have the same wife, and the same children. You may wish that you could cancel out the needs of the flesh, but you cannot. Sometimes I think that we get so carried away with the ecstasy of our spiritual experience that we expect even the things of the natural man to have changed, including our neighbors and family members.

Then, when we come to the realization that they have not changed, we start working on them; but not with God given wisdom! And we cannot understand why they do not see things the same way that we see them, and we try to force our experience upon them. Oh, for wisdom, for divine wisdom ! Make that a part of your daily prayer the very moment you open your eyes in the morning. Unfortunately, it is usually the folk who need wisdom most who do not see their lack of this divine gift.

I repeat. We are not only living a spiritual life but a bodily life. We are in a world with troubles and heartaches and sorrows. We are in the world — not of it — but we are still in the world. We must deal with a bodily life whether we like it or not, and a very large part of our time and interest is taken up with things which concern the body.

Kathryn Kuhlman

Day By Day

Now do not be misled into believing that this thing of victory is obtained once for all, a summit that is reached from which nothing can dislodge us. It is not something that you get all at once and then you sit back and rest in it, pull in your oars and say. Well, I've gotten a good dose of it now. I've been injected with this thing of victory and it is a once for all proposition !

It isn't like that at all! The very moment that simple faith is lost, in that moment is the victory over sin broken. And the sooner that you and I understand this fact, the better off we will be. If you are one of God's children, if you have been born again, if you are 'a Christian, then more than anything else you should desire this glorious victory. You yearn for victory over discouragement, the victory over sin, the victory over the enemy of your soul, the victory over temptation. There is nothing more thrilling than to live a consistent Christian life, moment by moment, with peace of mind and peace of soul.

I am not telling you that there will not be deep waters or troubles or problems. You see, I am so aware that we are a part of humanity, that there will be problems so long as we are in the flesh, that there will be troubles. Not only are there troubles, but the Word of God assures us of tribulations. I have them, and you have them, too. I don't care how deeply spiritual you may be this very hour, I still promise you that so long as you are a part of humanity, and you are in this flesh and still living in this world, there will be problems. You will have troubles. And that is the reason why I always say : "No matter what those troubles are, no matter what your discouragements might be, as long as God is still on His throne and hears and answers prayer (and you will remember that I never stop there. The whole responsibility is not God's. The next part is also vitally important) and as long as YOUR FAITH IN HIM is still intact, everything will come out all right !"

You know, so many of us like to put the whole responsibility on God and all we see is the bigness of God. That's thrilling and I could not agree more wholeheartedly. He is still God Almighty. His promises are true and they work. He has all power in heaven and on earth. He holds the key to every problem in that life of yours, but it is a two-way proposition : His part and your part. Your part is to have faith in Him, to have faith in His promises and belief that He will keep those promises. It is up to you to maintain a moment by moment walk of faith. Then, as long as your faith in Him and in His promises remains intact, you can say : All things work together for good (Romans 8 :28) . Then you know that you have victory in Christ. Then there will be peace of mind at all times, victory over temptation and over sin.

Sometimes I think that we feel we will forever rest on that wonderful summit, away up there on Pisgah's lofty mountain peak. Yes, it is a wonderful moment when God's Spirit bears witness with our spirit that we have passed from death unto life and we know that He has become our Heavenly Father, that we have entered into that relationship of father and child. But do not be deceived into believing that there will no longer be temptations, that there will be no moments of depression.

The victorious life is not something which is obtained once for all. This life of victory is secured through a moment by moment faith. There IS constant victory for the believer, but only so long as he trusts Christ entirely, and only for so long. The moment that simple faith is lost, then is victory over sin broken.

There must be that moment by moment, that day by day simple faith in Christ. That is why our Lord seems to sum up sin in just one word: unbelief. And the Scripture says, "The Holy Spirit, when he is come, will convict the world of sin ... of sin, because they believe not on me" (John 16:8, 9). And this is exactly why John writes : "This is the victory that over cometh the world, even our faith" (I John 5:4).

So, what is the victory that overcomes the world? FAITH! Since we are conscious of the fact there is no such thing as a once for all victory, it is evident that we must constantly be on guard because this earthly life is beset with perils. Or, to be strictly accurate, we must ever allow the peace of God to guard our hearts (Philippians 4:7). I once read of a man — an ordinary laborer — who used to quote that little verse in this way, "A PIECE of God shall guard your heart." I cannot argue with him. His idea was right. It is the indwelling Christ, the Son of God, who does this thing for us.

A long time ago, I came to the conclusion that defeat and not victory is the sad inscription which could be written over the life of many a follower of the Lord Jesus Christ. I meet them every day and I am sure you do, too. They wear a long face and it is evident that there is no victory and no real spiritual vitality there. If you are in their presence too long, their attitude begins to 'rub off' on you and you almost become depressed yourself. There is nothing gloomier than a professing Christian who is living in defeat.

The Word of God declares, "As thy days, so shall thy strength be" (Deuteronomy 33:25). He will not give you strength today for tomorrow's trials. Never. It is a day by day proposition. He will give you strength for today and for the difficulties that come to you today.

When I awaken in the morning, I have this confidence, I have this assurance, I have this security : that no matter what happens to me today, I know my Lord and my God will give me strength for what comes to me during those hours. Now, if I knew when I awaken in the morning everything that I would have to face in the next twenty-four hours, it would discourage me before I ever started out. I couldn't stand it. I couldn't take it. If I knew the disappointment that would come to my doorstep, or all the work that I would have to do, I would be tired before I began the day. If I had a preview of everything that was involved in the next eighteen to twenty hours, I would be tempted to crawl back in bed again, pull the cover over my face and say, I cannot take it !

But, I do not know what I will be faced with during those hours of that day. Yet, I go out secure. How? I leave with a trust and a confidence in my heart and in my mind that as that day, so will God supply the strength for that day. I have lived lo, these many years, without having a breakdown. People have nervous breakdowns when they try to see beyond that day. You cannot do it and be victorious. If right now I would stop and think of what my calendar looks like; if I were to visualize all my commitments on that calendar, all the services I have scheduled, all the telecasts and radio broadcasts I need to make, all the sermons I must preach .... If I would picture the load of daily mail before me, and all the prayer requests that await my attention on my desk, I would be defeated instantly and I might just as well say. Let somebody else take over for me ! But, I just don't do it. That is the reason I have never had a nervous breakdown. If you are on the verge of a breakdown, it's because you are trying to live more than one day at a time, more than one moment at a time. To live a victorious Christian life, do not cross the bridge until you get to that bridge. Do not ford those deep waters until you get to the brink of the stream. Do not lie awake at night and worry about that thing that you are going to have to do the next day. If you do, you will be so tired and such a nervous wreck the next day that when you face that task, you will not have the refreshed mentality or the rested body to do a good job.

So, go to bed and sleep and commit that thing to God. That's perfect trust. That's perfect confidence. That's where your faith in Him comes in. You sleep. If anybody is going to do the worrying, let God stay up and worry. Commit it to Him. If anybody has to work during the night, let God work so that when you awaken in the morning and you have to face that task, you are refreshed mentally and spiritually.

How in the world do you think I keep going? I do not believe anyone knows how much work I put out in one day, how long are my hours, or everything that I do. I could not be doing the work that I am doing if I did not live and practice the very things that I am telling you now.

If I have upset your theology a little by what I have said, let me remind you that if you have been taught one thing and the Bible says something different, the Bible is always right. If I say something and it is contrary to what is in the Bible, the Bible is right. If your church teaches something that is contrary to what the Bible says, the Bible is the very Word of God and it is absolute authority.

Now this thing of living the Christian life is simple, so simple that sometimes I think we feel the necessity to make of it a hard thing, when in reality it is something that should be very natural. The Christian life is the natural way to live. By this I do not mean that it is easy living a daily consistent Christian life; yet, it should not be a struggle and it will not be a life of struggle if you know how to live that life in Christ Jesus. A Christian should be the happiest person in the world, and you will be exactly that if you learn how to live this life of victory.

Confident Rest

Now that you have launched into this glorious new walk with Christ, consider some of the dangers that beset a life of holiness, this life of constant victory. There is such a thing for the Bible teaches it, and you must accept it if you believe the Word of God. But what are some of the hazards that challenge this wonderful life that the Word of God makes plain?

To be forewarned is to be forearmed. You need not fear to face any danger. You need not doubt in your heart that you will be able to live this life, or attain this daily consistent walk of victorious living. There is no reason for you to fear any danger for the Word of God says, "in ALL these things, we are more than conquerors through him that loved us." (Romans 8:37). Not only has Jesus made provision that all may become conquerors, and that we will be conquerors over anything and everything we face in life ..BUT MORE THAN CONQUERORS ! That's quite a promise ! And that promise comes from the highest authority in heaven and earth. Face it, accept it, and it will take away all fear.

First of all, it's human nature to try to live the life of victory by self effort. Please listen carefully to what I have to say here, for it may help you to cease from all your struggling and straining, and the terrific effort you are putting forth to be the kind of Christian you feel you should be in living this constant abiding life in Christ Jesus. If that describes your day-to-day existence then you will agree that it takes away most of the joy from your salvation, and the joy of being God's child. In fact, it takes the joy out of living!

In the first flush of ecstasy after Jesus has been received as Savior and Lord, realizing the impossibility of living such a life of victory without His help and powder, there is a tendency to 'hug' our possession, to make a continuous and conscious effort to cling to it lest we lose it. There is the feeling that if we do not strenuously concentrate our thoughts upon the indwelling Christ, maybe we will lose Him. We go to sleep at night feeling that we might lose ground even while we sleep. We awaken in the morning thinking that we must be very careful through that day and put forth every effort, lest we lose this wonderful experience or the nearness of the Master. I often wonder if this position comes from regarding the victorious life as a blessing or a possession we can forfeit or lose. I believe that Satan always tries to induce us to regard it as such. It is his plan to cause us to believe that it may slip from our grasp. But this is not so. It is not true !

Always keep in mind that we serve a Person, not a thing. This wonderful experience of being born again, this life of holiness, this walk of victory is a relationship with a Person, not a thing. It is the Lord Jesus Christ Himself who comes, not so much for us to possess Him, but that He may possess us. He cannot slip from our grasp. HE HOLDS US. He has promised, "I will never leave thee, nor forsake thee" (Hebrews 13:5). That is why I like to dwell upon the abiding Christ rather than the fullness of the Spirit. Someone put it so wisely:

Once it was the blessing, now it is the Lord ;

Once it was the feeling, but now it is His Word.

Once His gifts I wanted, now the Giver own.

Once I sought for healing, now I seek Himself alone."

That expresses exactly what I am talking to you about here. Jesus keeps us. It is not we who keep Him. "He," the Bible says (Jude 24) "is able to keep ..." He is able to keep you. He is able to keep me. We do not have to keep Him. Of course, we must allow the Lord Jesus Christ to be the home of our thoughts. We must be willing to be kept. That is where the danger comes in. The minute we are no longer willing for Him to keep us, then we get into trouble. But as long as we are willing for Him to keep us, then He is able to keep; and not only able, but willing, as long as we are willing to be kept in continuous victory.

I am talking to you about a life of victory, the provision made for a continuous and daily consistent Christian life of victory regardless of circumstances, regardless of depression, regardless of anything that might happen to you or come into your life. Looking unto Jesus in faith and love does not use or demand strenuous effort on your part to retain Him. He is a willing Savior. He is a willing Guest. He is a willing Lord. Your look of faith is not to be with strained eyes but with a restful gaze.

In the great miracle services in the First Presbyterian Church in Downtown Pittsburgh, so often I observe folk as they sit there in the pew, their faces etched with strain, their hands clenched into tight fists. They seem to be straining, straining to be healed, almost as though they are trying to heal themselves. It isn't like that. Rest entirely and completely in the Lord. Relax in His goodness. Then, in that moment as you are thinking about His bigness, the wonderful power of the Holy Spirit, and you are looking unto Jesus the Author and Finisher of your faith : suddenly you will feel that glorious presence of the Holy Spirit flowing through your body. It is not looking to Jesus through strained eyes, but with a restful gaze. It makes all the difference in the world.

"Abide in me," says our Lord in John 15:4. Rest peacefully in Him so far as your life of victory is concerned. At every alarm, at every approach of temptation, simply abide in Him. He is the Rock of Ages. He is all-powerful. "Consider the lilies of the field, how they grow" (Matthew 6:28). It is not by self effort nor by toiling and striving. They abide in the sunshine and they drink in its life. The Word of God reminds us : "Which of you by being anxious, by worry, by straining, can add one cubit to your stature?" (Matthew 6:27). In our Lord's mind was something more than physical stature. It is not our faith but His faithfulness that maintains the victorious life.

In the 37th Psalm, the 3rd Verse we read : 'Trust in the Lord, and do good ; so shalt thou dwell in the land, and verily thou shalt be fed." So very often I read this scripture from the pulpit during our Monday night services because I believe we need to hear this on Monday more than we do on Sunday ! It is through the week that we are confronted with all the problems and the difficulties. Trust in the Lord, trust in Him, do good. And you cannot trust in God without doing good for the two go hand-in-hand. You cannot separate the two. If you are not doing good, then there is something missing in your trust in the Lord ; for as surely as you are trusting in Him, you will invariably do good.

Then let us go on from there "So shalt thou dwell in the land and verily thou shalt be fed." In other words, the Lord will take care of you ! It's that simple ! I may remark in passing that even our conflict with evil around us — and I know the powers of the enemy are great, I know the temptations and the frustrations generated in this hour in which we live are many times ravaging — but even in view of these facts, our trust must be anchored entirely in Him and not in our own power or in our own efforts.

How remarkably this is brought out in our Lord's instructions to His disciples when He said, "Behold, I send you forth as sheep in the midst of wolves" (Matthew 10:16). Now look at this more closely. How does Jesus proceed? Does He say, Be ye therefore armed to the teeth? No, He doesn't say that! He continues by saying, "Be ye therefore harmless as doves." Why? Because He is our defense. He is our shield. Sometimes it is not easy to commit everything unto Him. It may not be easy to remain harmless as a dove and relax in Christ in your hour of frustration and with the circumstances under which you have to live. But, you can afford to relax because God is your defense and your shield, and in Him you are more than a conqueror !

Temptations

We have already seen that it is not self effort that insures this wonderful life of constant victory. Now may I point out another truth : that the victorious life is not an un-tempted life.

There are those who, after the wonderful new birth, following their experience of knowing that their sins are forgiven, living in the ecstasy of that transaction with the Lord Jesus Christ, have the notion that it is always going to be like that: without temptations or troubles. Perhaps I was the one who led them in the sinner's prayer and as they got up from their knees, their face still tearstained, I said to them : "Now remember to Whom you belong. You are an heir of God, a joint-heir with Christ Jesus.

You are somebody!" At a time such as that, it is easy to feel there will never again be temptations.

But life isn't like that ! You were converted but the

devil wasn't. You may feel as though the devil got converted, too ; but he is the same as he always was — and it's just like that.

Therefore, the Christian life is not an un-tempted life. Only one man has ever lived an unbroken victorious life, and that was our Lord and Savior Himself. And the Word of God states that Jesus was tempted in all points like as we are, yet without sin (Hebrews 4:15).

When someone stands behind the pulpit and teaches that there will no longer be temptations after this wonderful new birth experience, that one is unscriptural. Adam and Eve, created in a sinless state, were tempted and they also fell. So we need not be surprised that the devil tempts us. He will do all in his power to drag us down and he knows our weaknesses, he knows when we are tired, he knows when we are in a state of fatigue. He has no principles whatsoever. He will wait for that moment when we are vulnerable and it is then that he will strike.

The prophet Elijah knew that. At one moment he

was a great spiritual giant, challenging the prophets of Baal (I Kings 18). You and I think we have seen wonderful miracles but that was one of the greatest miracle services that ever took place. I'm sorry I missed it! You and I have seen sick bodies healed by the power of God, and we can right-fully say, Isn't that wonderful ! But I'll tell you something. Greater than anything you or I have experienced or witnessed was the occasion when Elijah stood before the prophets of Baal, challenging them in the name of the Lord, and God came through and sent the fire from heaven ! Had I been there while Elijah was defying the gods of the false prophets, I'm sure I would have been urging him on, standing behind him all the way, knowing that God always comes through with the victory.

But remember: it was only a few hours later, at a time when Elijah was weary in body and when his physical strength was gone, that temptation came. He was human and the devil was waiting for that weak moment to attack him. Just a few hours after that glorious victory on Mount Carmel, Elijah prayed to die. "Let me die! Jezebel is after my life," he cried!

How quickly and easily we, too, forget the power of our God when the enemy comes against us ! In that moment of Elijah's despair, did God cut him off? Did He forget or forsake him? No! No! He just let him sleep. God knew that all Elijah needed was twelve or fourteen hours of good, restful sleep ; and then He sent His angels to bake him a cake. That's what our Heavenly Father is like !

But I want you to see and never forget that the power of the enemy very often comes when our physical strength is weakest. The devil attacked Elijah when God's servant was tired in body and he assaulted him through the weakness of the flesh. There was no spiritual weakness, no weakness in the prophet's spirit. The weakness was in the flesh and God knew it. Therefore, let us not be surprised when Satan tempts us. He will do all in his power to drag us down because the victorious life is the only one that really counts. Thus, every child of God will be tempted. But we can count it all joy, even in the face of the temptation; for we are told that "the shield of faith is able to quench all the fiery darts of the evil one" (Ephesians 6:16). That is the reason why I say to you again :

No matter what happens, as long as God is still on

His throne and hears and answers prayer; and just so long as your faith in Him is intact, you cannot be defeated. YOU WILL NOT BE DEFEATED

Not one person needs ever go down in defeat as long as his faith in God is intact. And the most wonderful thing is that He will even supply the faith, for He is the Author and Finisher of our faith (Hebrews 12:2). He is the supplier of that faith, so how can we lose?

Perhaps right now you are defeated and you can see no possible path toward victory in your situation. Or maybe you are a backslider. Of course, under those circumstances, you are not having any spiritual results. You are not influencing your loved ones or the members of your church or those where you work. They can sense your defeat and all the while you long for a life of victory, the only life that really counts. Look up and by faith lay hold of the shield of faith. Do it now. Regardless of circumstances, the shield of faith is able to quench ALL the fiery darts of the evil one. If it wasn't true, God's Word never would have said it!

Snares and Pitfalls

In continuing our examination of the pitfalls before us in our Christian walk, it has been my observation that an awful lot of people have negative thoughts. They live a negative life and everything about them oozes with the contrary environment which they create. Whenever you are unfortunate enough to walk into their presence, even before a word is spoken, you feel the downward pull of their attitude and you wonder, What is it?

Don't be a negative person ! Don't practice a constant attitude of defeat thinking that you might fail, so you won't even try. Or, you won't ask because you might be refused; you won't make a request lest you be embarrassed by having someone say, No. Therefore, you remain passive and as the old saying goes. You sit in your rocking chair and you stay there all your life. Finally, when your last day comes, you find that you have never tried to do one thing simply because you were afraid of defeat, afraid of refusal. Get up out of that chair now! Say aloud, I'll try it! And I guarantee that you will be surprised at the results of your efforts.

You may be thinking that it's easy for me to say that. But do you know why I can make such a statement? Because that is the kind of life I have lived all of my days. I have lived that kind of existence because I refused to fix my eyes on people. Instead, I have fastened my attention on God, and in Him there are no limitations and in His promises there is no defeat.

I am zeroing in on someone right now who has made excuses for not being a Christian because of the fear that he might not be able to live the Christian life. You point to all the hypocrites that you have encountered and you talk about their failures. Do you know something? I give those hypocrites more credit than I give you. Why? Because they put forth an effort. You haven't even begun. Don't talk about those whom you label 'hypocrites.' They have done more than you have done. At least they put forth some effort and you have not done a thing!

Remember : as long as you and I are in the flesh, there is always the possibility of temptation and there will always be the possibility of sinning. We read in the Old Testament, in Leviticus 4 :3 — "If the priest that is anointed do sin as the people..." You may never have thought of a priest sinning but knowing human nature and man's weaknesses, God made provision for everyone, even those whom He anointed. Simply because you or someone else has been anointed of God and called of Him, does not mean that there will never be temptation or the opportunity to sin. God has made this fact very clear. In this case He speaks of the priest whom He has anointed , . . "And if he do sin . . ."

It is apparent here that sin is inevitable no matter who the person is. If you are a part of humanity then it is possible for you to sin. But, the most thrilling fact is that the Lord has made provision IF you sin. He has made provision for me if I sin. He has made provision for all if we should sin. Therefore, that person who says that he cannot be a Christian because maybe he won't be able to 'hold out,' is hiding behind a very feeble excuse. Get your eyes on the provision and not the possibility of sinning. God the Father thought of everything. He didn't forget a single thing. He understands the weaknesses of the flesh. He created us. He knows all about us, better than we know ourselves. Thus, He has made every provision — even if we sin.

For the sake of clarity, let me make an analogy. Every ship that sails the seas is provided with an adequate supply of life boats lest there be a wreck or collision. It doesn't matter how small or how large the ship, it is always provided with lifeboats because there is the possibility of a storm or a ultimate shipwreck. Of course, this does not imply that it is the Captain's intention to wreck his ship ; but provision is made because there is always the possibility of a disaster. And God, who is a wise and never-failing Heavenly Father, has made full provision for His children lest we sin !

In an earlier chapter, I pointed out that the victorious life is secured by an act of faith and this wonderful daily walk of triumph is maintained by a constant attitude of faith. There must be that unwavering trust in the Lord Jesus Christ.

Suppose then that there is a failure and you or I, in a moment of temptation, should yield to that temptation? What if, in that instant of crisis, we should give in to satanic pressures? There is the possibility that anyone of us can yield ; but there may be those who will counter this statement by attesting, "I have been filled with the Holy Spirit. I have spoken in tongues. I have this gift or that gift of the Spirit. I belong to an organization where we do not believe in sin!"

Contrary to those who take that stand, I have found that in the Body of Christ made up of human beings who are still in a body of flesh, it is possible for any man or woman to yield to temptation and thereby sin. There are no exceptions for the very Son of God was tempted in all points like as we are, yet He remained without sin (Hebrews 4:15).

Yes, you may be filled with the Holy Spirit, you may have received the baptism of the Holy Ghost, you may have spoken in tongues and God may have entrusted to you several gifts of the Spirit . . . but you are still open to attacks of Satan. Sometimes I think the folk to whom much has been entrusted are those that the enemy of our soul besieges most tirelessly.

Walk carefully. Walk softly. Guard well that which you have. If you are Spirit-filled, if God has bestowed on you heavenly gifts, if you have had great spiritual experiences, guard these things carefully for you are the very person that the enemy will attack. The more deeply spiritual you are, the greater will be the attacks of Satan upon you because you have greater influence than that one who is a weak Christian.

That is only logical. If the enemy can trip a spiritual giant and halt his effectiveness for God, that is exactly his plan. That person who has little or no influence for Christ, even though he is born again and has had that spiritual experience with the Savior, will not encounter the same measure of temptation as the one living close to Jesus. If the enemy is able to lure that borderline Christian into yielding to temptation, his victory will be small. It cannot compare to his delight in causing to falter that somebody whose spiritual influence is great. Therefore, we must be careful. We must walk softly. We must not be boastful but guard that faith well for the victorious life is secured by an act of faith ; and it is maintained only by a constant attitude of faith.

Let's face facts. What happens when there is a failure and you do fall into sin? What then? I can tell you right now, Satan will immediately follow up his victory by trying to persuade you that there is no such thing as the victorious life ; or if there is, that you never had the blessing of God in the first place. Or, he may cause you to believe that God's blessing is gone forever and you have lost it eternally.

There are those of you who read these words and say, "Kathryn Kuhlman, how do you know that much about me?" I don't, but I know exactly how the enemy works, and if he can convince you that you did not have salvation in the first place, he has won a big victory. If he can convince you that you have never been filled with the Spirit, he has won a double victory. If he can persuade you that you have never been called of God to your particular task, he has won a tremendous victory. He will try to put doubts in your mind. And remember, doubts are not of the Holy Spirit. Doubts are not of God, doubts come from the devil, the enemy of your soul. Defeat and depression are never of God. Oppression is never of God. Anything negative is not of God! Victory is God's language and we are MORE THAN CONQUERORS through Christ who loves us !

So, immediately after you have yielded to temptation, Satan comes and lays on you his 'guilt trip' and says, "Now you are ruined. You are absolutely ruined. Your testimony is of no effect. What will your family think? What will the folk in the church think? What will your friends think?" And you experience the desolation of defeat. You hang your head, your feet drag and you are the most miserable person in the world.

You may be a missionary having done a tremendous job for God on the mission field. But something has happened to you out there, or something has happened to a member of your family and the enemy of your soul is taking advantage and is doing a good job of convincing you that you have ruined everything, that you have lost your influence. If he can get you off the track, off the mission field and get you back home again in a little rented house and can get you to live the rest of your life in defeat and discouragement, he has won a mighty big victory. Think of all those souls that will never hear of the Lord Jesus Christ if you yield to defeat, if Satan is able to thwart your labors for the Master!

Right now, get up and start doing something about it ! But you say, "What can I do?" In the first place remember something: when a sin is confessed, it is forgiven (I John 1:9). Do not listen to Satan or to those who may accuse you. The Bible is full of victorious teaching. Victory was taught by Christ and it is revealed again and again in Paul's epistles and those of John. Remember that God gave us the victorious life after many, many falls (failures). Will He then withhold it forever because of one more fall? No!

"Then came Peter to Jesus, and said. Lord, how oft shall my brother sin against me, and I forgive him? till seven times? Jesus saith unto him, I say not unto thee, Until seven times : but. Until seventy times seven" (Matthew 18:21, 22). Jesus Himself gave the answer when Peter asked how many times he should forgive his brother if he sin against him. Once? Or maybe a second time? At the most, Lord, seven times (stretching his power for forgiveness) ? What does the scripture say? "Seventy times seven !"

We are to keep on forgiving again and again as long as that one comes and confesses it and asks forgiveness. If the Master restricted His forgiveness and if He promised to forgive us only once — or to forgive us not more than five, six or seven times at the most — all of us would be sunk. You cannot find in the Word of God where God's forgiveness is limited. He will not withhold His forgiveness from you ! But, if Satan can whisper to you and convince you that you cannot be forgiven, he will do it. Then, he has won a great victory.

Now we have conclusively shown that there is no striving, no struggling on our part to receive forgiveness or maintain the victorious life. It is the mercy of the Lord Jesus Christ. His mercy and grace. Therefore, it must be obvious that our efforts and struggling will never reinstate us should we sin. If we

fall into any sin, our Savior wishes us to turn to Him at once in faith for forgiveness. Do it immediately. The very second that you are conscious of sin, ask God's forgiveness and instantly He will put away your sin ! The minute sin is confessed, that moment your sin is put away. Praise God!

Other Dangers

Now, let's get very practical and regard something that is rarely discussed. Do not make the mistake to assume infallibility. You may ask, What in the world do you mean by that? Or you may consider such counsel as ridiculous. There will also be those who will say, I wouldn't think of assuming that I am infallible !

But wait a minute. There is a real danger of this in both your life and mine. I am very well aware that there is great joy in unbroken communion with our Lord and often a glorious consciousness of the indwelling Christ's power and presence. But it is not our power, it is His ; and I want you to see that there is a danger of our supposing that we always know God's will in any matter. Therefore, we may think that we are always right.

Have you ever met folk who are so spiritual that they are dead sure they can never make a mistake? Of course you have! They are so sure of the indwelling presence of Christ, they are so sure of their knowledge of the Word of God, they are so sure of their relationship with Him, they are so sure that they are infallible in making any decision that it becomes a danger.

I once read the account of a very marvelous Christian gentleman who told of an occasion when he lived with four devoted men of God. All were consecrated Christians and all were far more experienced in holy living than himself. Among them was one who was deeply taught from the scriptures. He consistently spent long hours alone in prayer ; and he, therefore, assumed that in all things and situations he had the mind of Christ. He was also of the opinion that any proposals which conflicted with his ideas must certainly be wrong. He was confident that he had to be right at all times because he spent so much time in prayer with the Father. He took for granted that he was a little more spiritual than the others. And it is true that sometimes he was right, but sometimes he was wrong! We need to remember that no matter how spiritual any of us might be, there are times when we can be wrong for we are still human and nobody is right all the time.

One morning, he very quietly stated, "I want you gentlemen to know that in this instance you will have to deem my decision as accurate and true because I have spent more time than any of you alone with the Master, and I know I am right."

One of the group spoke up and said, "My dear Jim, some of us think that we also are led of God. Do not misunderstand me. Remember, we all can be wrong because, as human beings, we are fallible. There is only One who is infallible and that is Jesus Christ."

That particular man always assumed that he was absolutely guided by God in all his proposals. But that is not always the case nor is it true. I have learned through the years that all of us are sometimes a little 'deaf spiritually, and we do not always clearly hear God's message, just as the physically deaf person does not always hear perfectly over the telephone. Perhaps you know someone who is a little hard of hearing and when that one answers the telephone, he is liable to make a mistake because of his hearing impairment.

So it is also true that we are a little deaf spiritually at times. There must be a perfect doing of God's Will before there is a perfect knowing of His doctrine. We need to recognize that we are all fallible, that we may be mistaken sometimes. I do not mean to infer, however, that the majority vote is always right even though the majority generally rules. Remember the Thirteenth Chapter of Numbers regarding the twelve leaders that Moses sent into Kadesh-barnea to spy out the Promised Land. Only two brought back a favorable report while ten men said, "We are not able to go up against the people for they are stronger than we" (Verse 31). If the majority is always right then the ten spies would have been right. They were the majority. No, only two were confident of success and said, "Let us go up at once, and possess it; for we are well able to overcome it" (Verse 30). Unfortunately, the people sided with the ten, and forty years of wandering, of misery and rebellion ensued because they did not heed the advice of the two who had the mind of God and were right. But again I remind you and I say to myself as well : do not assume infallibility. Any one of us can be wrong regardless of how spiritual we may be.

I guarantee that what I am sharing with you is very practical, for I am dealing with everyday problems, the things we must all face and the trials that help us to grow to spiritual maturity. Perhaps these situations are not among those often discussed for I am quite conscious that most folk like to hear about the wonderful mountain-top experiences which are indeed glorious. All of us like messages regarding the Holy Spirit who is our Helper and our Strengthener. But remember, even after a wonderful mountain- top experience such as Peter, James and John had when they saw Jesus transfigured before their very eyes, and Moses and Elijah stood before them they had to come down the mountain, down to good practical everyday living.

We cannot ignore this world although we are cautioned not to become part of it; but we are still in the world, our existence is in the world. Jesus Himself said exactly that when in His prayer He said: "Father ... I pray not that thou shouldest take them out of the world, but that thou shouldest keep them from the evil (one)" (John 17:15). We are not to become a part

OF the world, but that does not mean that we are not IN the world. We are! We are in the world and we cannot close our eyes and ignore it.

A father had a question concerning his little boy and he asked me, "Do you think it is wrong if I play marbles with my four-year-old son?"

What a question ! The father was a Christian, a saint of God and perhaps someone pointed a critical finger at him for playing a game of marbles with his child. But I knew in that moment it would delight the heart of Satan if he could persuade this man, and other holy people, that all pleasure is sinful. There are some folk who feel that way.

I replied to his query : "Dear man of God : by all means play marbles with your little boy, if you are not tempted to cheat. And if you are tempted to cheat, only then that seemingly harmless game becomes sin to you."

In spite of how innocent any situation may appear,

we can always make sin out of it. I don't care what it is, you can make sin of anything. We are living not only a spiritual life, but a bodily life and whether we like it or not, a very large part of our time and interest is taken up with things that concern the body.

It has become apparent to me that those who are living the victorious life are the happiest, the most human of all people on earth ; and they overflow with the joy of the Lord, and are the most delightful people to be with. I firmly believe that God's children should be the happiest people in the whole world. I believe that it is very inconsistent that a Christian should go around with a long face or displaying a depressed attitude. Just to be in the presence of someone like that brings down a spirit of depression. I do not want to be around people who cannot smile, who do not have the joy of the Lord. This is a wonderful world that God has given to us and this thing of living the Christian life is a wonderful life. We can still smile in spite of our circumstances. 'The joy of the Lord is our strength!" (Nehemiah 8:10).

The Bible also tells us to "rejoice evermore" (I Thessalonians 5:16), and that means NOW . . . that we are to begin NOW while we are on this earth. I do not see how these people who always seem to wear a long face are going to enjoy heaven. That's true! There is going to be laughter there, it's eternal joy in heaven. Stop to think of something else : we do not have to wait until after death has come to become the sons of God. No, "Beloved, now are we the sons of God" (I John 3:2). Right now! This very moment! I am still here on earth in bodily form. I am in the flesh in the world; yet, I am a child of God now. I do not have to wait until I get home to heaven to be a child of God or to be happy and to rejoice. The joy of the Lord is my strength NOW at this very moment.

I challenge you, therefore, to start enjoying your inheritance in Christ Jesus now. You need not wait another moment. Take Him at His word !

God, Our Provider

I hope and pray with all of my heart that you have accepted the challenge I made at the close of the last chapter : to start enjoying your inheritance as God's precious child ; and now I urge you to accept another of His provisions, one found in the Second Book of Kings, the last chapter, the last verse (II Kings 25:30) : "A daily rate for every day of your life, so long as you shall live." I have literally lived by that promise. I have claimed that promise for years and years. A daily rate, not a weekly rate, nor a monthly rate. Not a contract for five or ten years. It is God's guarantee of a daily rate every day of my life and yours so long as we both shall live !

If you are worrying about your finances, if circumstances have stripped you of a regular income, if your mate has died and you are suddenly faced with earning a living, or you may have been forced to assume the position of head of your household, of both mother and father to your children : remember, you are not alone ! Your Heavenly Father knows all about your problems and needs and He has promised a daily rate for the rest of your life. You won't 'go under' in defeat ! No, not if you have the same Heavenly Father that I have, and I am sure you do. Your Heavenly Father is my Heavenly Father. My Heavenly Father is your Heavenly Father. There is just one God and either you believe His Word or you don't.

The Bible here states that a daily rate will be given you of the King. Who is the King? Why our Heavenly Father! If that isn't security I don't know what security is. Many people turn to the government for their security and no one can be sure that those checks will continue to come every month. That's not real security. I can point you to One who can give you better security than even the government. Do you realize that the United States Government can go bankrupt? Who ever thought that the Pennsylvania Railroad would file bankruptcy? If my Papa knew that the Pennsylvania Railroad went bankrupt, he would turn over in his grave ! There was a day when it was believed that the railroad would be the last institution to lose financial credibility. But they did! Our real security is in Christ Jesus. I am secure in something that IS secure and as a child of God, you can be secure in something that is REAL security. God will never go bankrupt. Never, never, never!

We need to be reminded that the church of Jesus Christ is not a certain denomination, neither is it an institution. Jesus Christ Himself is the head of His church ; He is the head of His body of believers. This invisible church with Christ as the central figure will never go bankrupt. His church will never know defeat because He is the head of His church. If you are a part of that invisible body of believers, you can be assured that you need never go down in defeat. You are guaranteed spiritual wealth and victory if you are a part of this invisible body.

And so it is, beloved, with your trust and your confidence in Him, you can live in constant victory. Not for one minute do you have to worry about poverty or failure because your King has promised you a daily rate all the days of your life even if you live to be a hundred years old! You'll never live too long and no night will be too dark. You do not have to be overcome by any burden. Just remember to Whom you belong; and because you are living a moment by moment and a day by day kind of life, you will find that you are a happy person. I still contend that people living the victorious Christian life are the happiest and most human of all people living. They possess a special kind of joy, not something that is forced, but a joy that is spontaneous. It saddens me when I see an unhappy Christian for I know they are missing God's best blessings, that there is something wrong in their life. Your circumstances, however dire they may be, make no difference.

God has made provision for you to be happy because the Word of God continually speaks of the joy of the Lord and that promise which I gave you earlier (Nehemiah 8:10) is profound — "The joy of the Lord is your strength." I know what these words really mean. The joy of the Lord that He gives me empowers me to serve Him, the joy that I receive from helping others is my strength. It is something that neither you nor science can analyze but it is something that is as real as the air you breathe. No one will ever know the joy that I get out of helping others. No one will ever know. No one will ever know the joy that is mine as I give. I receive a far greater thrill, a far greater joy out of giving than perhaps the joy and pleasure that the folk experience who are recipients of the gifts. Inside of me I feel a sense of deep gratitude and happiness. It is a glorious world. It is a glorious life. It is so challenging and rewarding.

Some time ago God gave the people of the Kathryn Kuhlman Foundation the opportunity to minister to the needs of the people of Viet Nam. I don't know if those people got as big a thrill out of receiving from us as the joy that was ours from giving to them. I have been so excited about the hospital that this ministry is building there. I have personally experienced a greater thrill by our providing the supplies — the hospital beds, the sheets and pillow cases, the wheelchairs for the amputees — than if we were furnishing a magnificent home some place. I can visualize the bodily comfort that these sick folk are finding, and the spiritual blessings that are theirs as they learn of the Savior's love for them. I am reminded of the many who will benefit from the water pumped by the wells we have perhaps for the very first time in some of their lives.

Do you understand what I am trying to say? If you don't, that may be one of the reasons why you are not a happy Christian. That is possibly the reason why you have never experienced the real joy in being a Christian. Love is something you do ! It is something that is spontaneous.

If you have to force yourself to live the kind of life that I am talking about, then you have never had that experience where you have literally become a part of God and God has become a part of you. If you have to force yourself, then there is something wrong. You are not a part of Jesus, and Jesus is not a part of you. There is a place where literally your vitality comes from Him, and His vitality flows through your body. You take on the personality of Jesus. You cannot help it. You take on the personality of Jesus and the joy of the Lord becomes your strength. It is inescapable !

Holiness

This discussion is about something that is seldom brought to our attention. I am not sure if it's because we do not realize its importance, or if there is another reason; but it is undoubtedly a subject worthy of our prime concern.

A young Christian mother sat searching her Bible. She continued to spend much of the day reading, seeking out the deeper things of the Spirit. She was so hungry for His baptism and through the Word of God she was attempting to find the key in order to receive this blessing from God. She spent many hours seeking and examining the scriptures, so many in fact, that her household duties became tiresome and tedious and they were either hurried through or many times entirely neglected. The former peace and warmth and homeyness that had made their home a haven for the entire family were gone.

One day, as she was very deep in study, her little

girl toddled to her side carrying a broken doll. She said, "Mommy, please mend my dolly. Please?"

With an impatient gesture the mother pushed the little one aside and said, "I have more important things to do than to be troubled with your dolly. Go and play, honey. Can't you see that Mommy is busy with her Bible?"

The little one turned sadly away and the mother continued her search for holiness. But her search was a fruitless one and at last the mother closed the Bible with a sigh, and she sought the little child. She found her asleep with her little doll cuddled in her arms. Tears were still wet on her pretty little face.

God spoke to that mother right then and there. Instantly her heart was smitten with conviction, and she tenderly stooped over the little one, and caressed her with her kisses. Taking her in her arms, the mother breathed a prayer to God for forgiveness. To her child she said, "I am sorry, honey. Mommy will fix your dolly for you."

In that moment God revealed to that precious mother the fact that holiness could not thrive on neglected duties. Her devotion to her Lord was henceforth seen in her care of her family, her husband, her young daughter, her household ; and that house again became a home and the very pages of scripture were lighted up with a fresh glory.

    There is a holiness in being a good mother. There is a holiness in being a good wife. Holiness also means being a good husband. You cannot say that you are deeply spiritual and following the Lord in holiness if you are neglecting your children, if you are neglecting that son or daughter, that husband, that wife. I am saying something that is as practical as the Word of God. Do not neglect your family. Do not neglect your children. You are a living example to them. You may be the only Bible that they are reading right now. In neglecting them, they may lose confidence in you as a spiritual individual and a godly mother. Years later, they may point an accusing finger at you and say in truth, You were so busy reading the religious magazines and books that you did not have time to be an example of Christ or a Spirit-led mother to your family."

I am reminded of the daughter who came to me and asked, "Miss Kuhlman, do you have to teach fasting? Is it in the Bible? It is something that is causing trouble in our home and resentment within me."

I answered, "Yes, fasting is taught in the Bible. It is something that God honors ; but why do you resent fasting so much?"

I was not prepared for the look on this young girl's face. She was distressed and extremely troubled by what I had said. It was apparent that she had a valid reason to find 'fasting' so distasteful, and a reason to resent and even hate it. When she spoke the word she almost spoke it with vengeance.

I questioned her further, "Why do you hate fasting so much?"

She looked me straight in the eye and said, "I'll tell you exactly why, if you have time to listen."

Of course I had the time so she continued : "Every Friday my mother attends your miracle service at the First Presbyterian Church in Pittsburgh, and every

Friday is her fast day. When Friday morning comes, she makes all the family so miserable that we hate to gather at the breakfast table. I hate Friday! Dad hates Friday ! My little sister and brother hate to see Friday come because we know that when we sit down at the breakfast table. Mom will come in with a long face. She will pour Dad's coffee. She will serve our eggs and toast and cereal. But she will do it dutifully, with a long, sad face and with every gesture she will remind us that she is fasting, that she would love to have breakfast. But it's her consecration to fast !

"Then, she pours Dad's second cup of coffee which usually prompts a little sermon about fasting. Miss Kuhlman, for the sake of our family, couldn't you please leave out fasting in your teaching?"

I slipped my arm about this young lady and said, "Honey Bunch, I can't leave out something that is in the Word of God. It is your mother who has to learn to find joy in fasting. When fasting is drudgery and it is nothing more than a duty and a form and ceremony, it has lost its purpose. Your mother may just as well sit down at the breakfast table on Friday morning and eat two eggs instead of one, because fasting doesn't mean anything more to her than a form, a ceremony, a duty. The real joy has been taken out of her sacrifice and she is only making it a burden to her family and something they will despise all the rest of their lives."

Consider this as a warning given in love : if your family no longer regards their home as a haven, it is time to search your own life, to search your own heart. I am talking to God's children who profess spiritual things. Always remember : a man's home should be his castle ; and every man who has a family should be happy and desire to come home, to spend the evening with his wife and children.

It is the duty of the wife to create an atmosphere of peace and warmth and love, to bring about a special kind of homeyness that will prompt the husband and the children to hurry home. If your children prefer to be at the neighbor's house rather than their own home, there may be something wrong with the atmosphere of their home life and you will be wise to make it a matter of prayer.

When I was a child, I liked Mama's cookies better than the cookies that any neighbor baked, although I am not so sure Mama's cookies were that good. And I can still hear Mama apologize for the burnt toast that she often served Papa at breakfast. Then Papa would say, "Well, Emma, I would rather have your burnt toast than eat any place else."

I can remember our visits to Aunt Belle's house. Now my Aunt Belle was Mama's sister, and I might just as well tell you that Aunt Belle was a show-off. When we went to eat at Aunt Belle's, her table was loaded with a wide variety of good things. She would prepare several different kinds of meat and when it came to desserts, cake and pie were never enough. She always made something else, too.

But let me share something with you. The very next day after we had been to Aunt Belle's, Papa would turn to Mama as they sat at the supper table and say, Emma, I would rather eat at home any day than eat at Belle's house."

Now it wasn't because Mama was such a good cook. She really wasn't. She didn't like to cook. Mama was never a slave to her kitchen. I can see her now as she sat on the front porch swing. Supper time was getting near and suddenly Papa could be seen coming down the walk. Mama would turn to me and say,

"Quick! Quick! Quick, Kathryn! Put the tablecloth on the table and the coffee pot on the stove ! Here comes Papa!"

As long as Papa saw the white tablecloth on the table and the coffee pot on the stove, he didn't know but what Mama had slaved all day in order to prepare for supper that night.

A happy home goes far deeper than a meal on the table. Mama made a nice home. There was an atmosphere of love there, and we would rather be home, sit at our own supper table than anywhere else in the world. Papa would rather eat Mama's burnt toast for breakfast, I'd rather have Mama's cookies than any of the neighbor's cookies or any of Aunt Belle's food !

God has given us a physical frame which needs food, and it is also a part of His great plan for humanity that we work. God never expected us to be happy without work and He has so designed man that he is happiest when he works. It is no disgrace to work. It is a part of God's plan for a healthy human life.

We read that the Lord Jesus watched the children at their play and the fishermen and the farmers at their work. Jesus Himself worked, yet He took time to be present at a wedding feast in Cana. He wishes you and wishes me to take a genuine interest in all the concerns of life, and those of our friends. He has given us a capacity for pleasure and He long to see us enjoy His gift of life. What-ever we do, beloved, there must be joy in what we do.

God created us for work. He has made us for food, He has made us for exercise, He has also made us for relaxation. He wants us to enjoy our meals. He wants us to enjoy our work. He wants us to enjoy our recreation. He has fashioned the marvelous realm of nature —

"All things bright and beautiful,

All creatures great and small.

All things wise and wonderful,

The Lord hath made them all !"

And He has created all things for our pleasure as well as for His glory.

God expects His children to be careful about their dress and their manners. Surely He desires us to be attractive Christians. I remember how diligently Mama worked in order to make me nice little dresses. She would sew into the wee hours of the night, even after Papa had gone to bed. Why? Because she delighted in me. I was her child. She wanted me to look nice. She was proud of me.

And I firmly believe that our Heavenly Father wants you and me to dress and look and act so that He can be proud of us, proud enough to say, "That's My daughter! That's My son!" He wants that for you and me, too!

Mere Religion

Recently a lovely young lady, just twenty-three years old, flew into Pittsburgh from New York City for the purpose of attending the Friday service in First Presbyterian Church. Her family and all her relatives live in a southern city. The family is very religious and every member for generations has belonged to the same church. Even before each new baby would utter its first cry, they all knew in advance that when that baby was born, it would be taken to that church and when it got old enough, it would go to Sunday School in that church. And then when it reached the age for church membership, it would be a member of that church, and when it got a little older, it would sing in that choir. And finally as the young men grew to adulthood, they would become deacons or church officials. It was like that for generations.

But here, suddenly, this extremely brilliant college girl broke the pattern and became defiant. She was the first member of the family to turn her back on the church. When she arrived in Pittsburgh, I found her to be very rebellious ; but very frank and honest with me.

One of the first things she said to me was, "Miss Kuhlman, I rebel against religion. I'm sick and tired of it!"

Before she could go any further, I looked directly at her and I said, "Isn't it strange that you and I feel the same way?"

She stared at me with utter disbelief written across her face. I had taken her completely off guard, so much so that she was silent. She just looked at me with her mouth open. She didn't say a word even though her little speech wasn't finished.

"You heard me correctly," I said and added, "You know, if I had to be religious, I wouldn't be doing what I'm doing today because I'm not constituted in such a way that I can easily be religious. Even as a child I was the most mischievous kid in Concordia, Missouri. Joe Kuhlman's girl was unpredictable. There are some people, I believe, who are born religious ! They seem to be born good. Now you take my oldest sister Myrtle. I'm sure she was religious from her first breath. She was just naturally religious. It was natural for her to be good. How Papa and Mama ever got me, I'll never know, and God knows that they never quite figured it out either. I could not be a religious person if

I had to be. I'm sick of religion, too!"

This young girl was so shocked she still didn't say a word. But I continued, 'Do you want to know something? I'm just crazy about Jesus! I love Him so much! I love Jesus more than anything in the whole world because, you see, my whole life revolves not around religion, my whole life revolves around a PERSON, and that person is Jesus Christ, the Son of the Living God. I might just as well confess that I'm in love with Jesus!"

I went right on talking because she was still standing there, her mouth open. No one had ever talked to her like that. I said, "You see, if it was just a matter of being religious, I couldn't be doing the kind of thing that I'm doing. I do what I do, I work as hard as I work because of a person, and everything that I believe revolves around a person, the Person of God the Father, the Person of Jesus Christ the Son, the Person of the Holy Spirit. It isn't something that's cold, it isn't an institution, it isn't an organization, it isn't religion as such. It is something that is personal. It is something that is the most vital thing in my life. It is something that is alive. It is something that gives me a purpose for living, a purpose for doing. It gives real meaning to life ; and what I live is a life, and not just mere religion."

Finally, she retrieved her voice and we had a good long talk together. Before she left, she said, "I see the whole thing. Just pray for me now. Miss Kuhlman. Pray that I'll not miss God's best for my life !"

You see, God's religion never yet made a man miserable. Think that one through. Maybe all that you've had through the years is just religion. There are thousands of people that all on earth they ever had is religion, and just enough religion to make them miserable. They are having a terrible time, just an awful time being religious. Every Sunday morning our churches are filled with religious people, and in many instances even the one who stands behind the pulpit has nothing more or less than his religion. The Bible has never become alive to him. Jesus Christ has never really become a living personality to him. God the Father is still one that is very mystical, far off, he knows not where. You can perceive it in his prayers. He isn't quite sure to whom he is praying, whether or not he is really praying to a person, or if anyone at all is hearing his prayers. That is the reason why the Holy Spirit and the power of the Holy Spirit are never real to him.

The Holy Spirit can never get through to a person who is merely religious. There is a mighty big difference between religion and the Person of God the Father, the Person of Jesus Christ the Son, and the Person of the Holy Spirit !

May I ask you where you stand? Are you merely a religious person? If you are, you are not alone. There are tens of thousands exactly like you. But watch. If your life is centered around a person, you have something MORE than religion. You have a purpose for living. The Bible and God's Word are real to you. You have joy, you have peace of mind and God's religion never yet made a man miserable! Nor does the Lord Jesus Christ delight in misery !

It is amazing how many religious people have a theology all of their own, a doctrine all of their own, and it includes the fact that God delights in misery and in making people miserable. Did not the Savior Himself say, 'These things have I spoken unto you, that my joy might remain in you, and that your joy might be full" (John 15 :11) ? Cold religion does not give joy.

Now remember, there is a right way of making the most of both worlds. One way is right. Any other way is wrong. If your life revolves around the person of Jesus, not simply as an influence, not as a wonderful example, but the person of Jesus as the very Son of the living God who forgives your sin. One who hears the cry from your heart, then yours is not mere cold religion.

How can you know anything but victory when you are assured that there is a person who ever lives to make intercession for you, a great High Priest, One who is interested in you as an individual? Mere religion does not give you a great High Priest, an Advocate, One who left you His Name to use before He went away. Jesus said, "Here, I give you my name to use, and when you come into the presence of the holy Father, present my name. Come in my name before the throne of One who is absolute perfection. absolute holiness and you will have a hearing." (John 14:13-14; John 15:16; John 16:23,26,27)

Religion doesn't do that for you. Religion is cold. Religion is something abstract. There is no warmth or love in religion. There is no real strength in religion. It won't stand the test when you come face to face with temptation. It will not stand the test when you come face to face with disappointment. It will not stand the test when you come face to face with the open grave or eternity.

Do not rely on mere religion. If you do, it will never stand the test. The Heavenly Father is a person, Jesus Christ is a person and the Holy Spirit is a person. True Christianity is not religion, it is a relationship with the Persons of the Trinity : the Father, the Son and the Holy Spirit.

Feelings

As we begin to examine this thing of 'feelings,' let me stress the proper order : fact comes first, faith is second, and feelings are third. They should always remain in that order. We all have feelings for we are part of the human race ; but I caution you lest you allow your life to be governed solely by your feelings. Too many people rely on feelings, just feelings alone.

There are literally thousands of thousands who have experienced the ecstasy, the thrill of having been born again. They know that their experience is real, as real as God Himself, as real as the person of Jesus Christ.

But let me remind you that one's feelings, the ecstasy, the thrill of salvation have absolutely nothing to do with the facts. You are saved by fact, saved by the promises of the Word of God, saved because of the price that Jesus paid for you on the cross. You accept the pardon, you accept what Jesus did for you BY FAITH and by faith alone.

The fact is, we were born in sin. Then Jesus came and died on the cross. He paid the price in full by His death, and we reach out and accept that for ourselves personally. Jesus bought and paid for the whole thing. All we have to do is reach out and personally accept what He has already bought and paid for in our behalf.

Feelings are not always involved when a decision to receive Christ is made. In many instances, yes. But not always. I have seen some folk respond to an altar call time after time. I have asked them the question: "Didn't you come before? Why do you come again?"

Invariably the answer I received went something like this, "Well, I didn't FEEL I was saved. I didn't FEEL that my sins were forgiven."

Feeling has nothing to do with it whatsoever! You are saved on facts and the moment, by faith, you accept what Jesus did for you — you accept His pardon — it is done. The Word of God clearly states in I John 1:9, "If we confess our sins, he is faithful and just to forgive us our sins." The very minute you confess, that moment it is done whether or not there are any feelings involved.

We all know folk who, when they get up in the morning and if they do not feel well or failed to get a good night's sleep, are certain that God has turned His back on them and the Bible is not true. Everything spiritual that they possessed leaked out as they slept. They are like a deflated balloon, and they mope around all day, good for nothing, not even to God. Why? Because everything in their life, whether they are up or down, depends on their feelings. When they feel 'down,' they make life miserable for their family, for their neighbors, for everyone with whom they come in contact. But, if their feelings are 'good,' they have victory. Everything hinges on how they feel.

You are saved by fact, but the 'feelings' will eventually come. You will experience the ecstasy and the joy when you realize you have passed from death unto life, when you realize that God is your Heavenly Father now, when you realize that your sins are forgiven and that you do not have to stand before God in judgment and give an account of your sins that were all forgiven at the moment of your new birth. If that doesn't make you happy and bring you real joy and ecstasy, nothing will.

God wants us to trust Him. He wants us to trust His Word and not to rely upon feelings. He would save us from the peril of testing our victory, or testing His indwelling by any preconceived notion of ours as to how His presence should be felt or manifested. Think less of the victory, less of the blessing and MORE of the Blesser. I always smile at what Mr. Spurgeon said and I think of it so very often. It's worth repeating here. His words were wise when he said,

"I looked to Jesus and the Dove of

Peace flew into my heart. I looked

at the Dove of Peace and she flew away!"

Focus your attention upon Jesus. When you look to Jesus, He will give you that wonderful peace. His Dove of Peace.

Now faith is not something tangible that you can carry in your pocket and reach down and take it out, examine it, then put it back again. Neither is your salvation something that you keep in a little bag, open it, take it out, look at it and then put it back again. No! Salvation is a life. Victory over sin is a life. Being filled with the Holy Spirit is more than one definite experience for five or ten or fifteen minutes. It, too, is a life. Therefore, do not examine or test your victory, but just maintain a simple and constant trust in God. It is a day by day, an hour by hour, a moment by moment living in Him, knowing that He cannot and He will not fail.

Sometimes I think it is really better to enter into the victorious life by simple faith, unaccompanied by ecstasy or thrills, but this is not always the case. I'm sure you have heard people talk about the feeling that accompanied their born again experience — mine was like that.

I will never forget the Sunday morning when I, a fourteen-year-old girl, in a little Methodist Church in Concordia, Missouri, had my first encounter with Jesus. I have never doubted that experience all through these years, neither will I forget the thrill that was mine. There was an ecstasy, a definite feeling I had never known before and when I left that church and started for home, I really felt that every house I passed had just gotten a brand new paint job! They hadn't. They were just as much in need of paint as they were when I passed them on my way to church that morning. They just looked freshly painted to me. All the way home, after that wonderful experience, even the grass seemed to be greener. My feet barely touched the pavement.

Had I expected nothing more and had I leaned on the ecstasy of that single experience for the rest of my life, I would have been sunk. Since that time, I am frank to tell you, there have been some nights that have been mighty black. There have been some waters that have been mighty deep. There have been days when I have literally had to take the presence of Jesus by faith alone. Yes, you may know exactly what Fm talking about. There hasn't always been that feeling of ecstasy. Let me remind you that the absence of the thrill and the ecstasy does not prove that Jesus has left you or that you are alone. God wants us to learn to trust Him and trust His Word, and not to rely upon mere feelings.

I add something here because it is vitally important. Do not adopt the habit of constantly talking about Satan. I get so sick and tired and depressed by these people who begin talking about Satan as soon as you come into their presence : how he did this or that. They are dead sure that it was Satan in the life of their husband that prompted his actions, or who brought sickness into the home, or caused hard feelings with a loved one.

No one believes more than I do in the reality of Satan and his power. He is real. His power is real. But instead of talking about Satan, talk about Jesus! If you continually talk about Satan, a spirit of depression will descend upon your own life. It will permeate your home, and anyone entering your doors will sense that spirit of depression. You will be responsible for having brought that spirit into your home because you allowed Satan to rule your mind and thinking, and finally to rule you.

Instead, keep your eyes on Jesus ! Keep your mind on Jesus. Maintain a simple and constant trust in Christ. He cannot fail. Were it possible for us to make a choice, it would be far better to enter into the victorious life by simple faith in Christ unaccompanied by ecstasy or thrill; for when the thrill subsides and life seems humdrum and commonplace, we may be tempted to think the victory has vanished with the thrill. Do not trust feelings whatever you do ! Be careful to place fact first — then faith — then feeling. Follow that order and you will never live a defeated Christian life.

With Your Eyes on Jesus

Previously we discussed 'feelings' and how they can affect your victory. But now another matter needs to be dealt with since you have embarked on the life of surrender to God. DO NOT BE SURPRISED IF OTHERS FAIL TO SEE YOUR VICTORY!

I can remember what a precious Jewess said when she gave her testimony. She confessed, "When I found Christ as my Savior in Carnegie Auditorium in Pittsburgh, it was such a glorious experience I thought that my husband and my whole family would rush to follow my example and have the same experience that I had. No one was more surprised than I when they just looked at me — they didn't believe me! They thought I had 'gone off the deep end!' I rationalized and excused them because of love and knowing that families are sometimes stubborn and difficult.

"But my friends ... I knew they were different, that they were intelligent and had confidence in my judgment. When I would tell them about my experience with Jesus, they would understand; and I was sure they would waste no time to attend a service and receive the same blessing that I now had."

Then she admitted, "Lo and behold, they weren't moved at all ! I have to confess that I was almost critical regarding my husband and my family, and it was difficult for me to believe that my friends reacted in the same way."

Remember something. Only one man ever lived a sinless, a really victorious life all through his days on earth and that is the man Christ Jesus. But His contemporaries, the leaders of religion, were so blinded that they failed to see the victorious life in Jesus. So they called Him a winebibber, a sinner and accused Him of having a devil. They had no understanding whatsoever of the perfection in the life of Jesus. Their spiritual vision was so obscured that they did not recognize that He was the very Son of the living God.

They said of Jesus, "We know that this man is a sinner" (John 9:16, 24) ; and so we must not be surprised if men fail to recognize the victorious life in us. If this is the case, just smile. Never fight back. Continue to be humble. Humility is one of the greatest of all Christian graces, and there is nothing more convincing to an unbeliever than the fruits of a victorious life in Christ Jesus, the life of one who is following the Master.

When others oppress us or when they deny our sincerity or when they say we are not orthodox, we must not give vent to a spirit of un-love nor allow a root of bitterness to come in. And be careful lest you present a 'holier than thou' attitude. Should you entertain an emotion such as that for even one minute, your victory is broken and your influence will be lost. There is nothing more disgusting or nauseating to others than one who professes to be a Christian, yet manifests such a spirit.

Permit me to go a step farther. I direct a word of caution to those who have been filled with the Holy Spirit and have received the Baptism : be careful that you do not display an attitude of spiritual bigotry. Bigotry is not a character trait of the Holy Spirit . . . but humility is.

If Jesus, the very Son of the living God, chose to set us an example by His willingness to become a servant, girding Himself with a towel and washing the dusty feet of His disciples; then surely we who have been filled with His Spirit must live to serve and manifest the humility of our Lord and our Savior who equips us with power for service.

Do not wait for future opportunities to manifest the indwelling Christ, looking for a very special occasion to arise, expecting a big moment to testify to the power of Jesus, to be heard publicly as you stand before a large gathering.

I am constantly aware that my ministry is not limited to public services. The services stay secondary. My greatest opportunities to witness for Jesus are NOW in my contact with the garage attendant, with the waitress in the restaurant, the grocery clerk and even those who work with me in the office. For me to live is Christ . . . and He is love !

Let It Shine

As we go a step farther, turn to a portion of the Word of God found in the Sixth Chapter of Romans, the Twenty second Verse, where we again see the same word 'now,' which we encountered earlier.

"But NOW being made free from sin, and become servants to God, ye have your fruit unto holiness, and the end everlasting life.

Isn't that thrilling? We know that the only time that we can live this victorious life is right now and the only way to have victory through Christ is to take it now at this very moment. You see, not one of us is assured of the moment beyond this moment. I am not assured of the week beyond this week. I am not assured of the month beyond this month.

I have only the assurance of this moment; therefore, I must take advantage of every opportunity that this moment holds for me.

The most important element in the world is time. There is nothing that is more important to you or me at this moment than time, for when time is gone, all the powers on earth and in heaven cannot bring it back again. Think of it, while you have been reading these words, those moments are now history and you cannot bring those moments back again. Since you awakened this morning, those hours are now history. All the powers on earth, all the powers in heaven, God Himself cannot bring those hours back again to you and those hours were filled with opportunities. That all important element of time is the most important element in the world to you.

If you are a wise person, you will realize that every moment has its opportunity and you will take advantage of those opportunities now. God is light as well as love, and our Lord said, "Let your light shine" (Matthew 5:16). He did not say to make it shine as occasion arises. We are to let it shine always and everywhere, every moment of every hour and every hour of every day. If you are a Christian, if you are among those who are sons of God, heirs with Christ and heirs of God, joint-heirs with God's only begotten

Son, you are to let your light shine . . . not for an hour a day, not for thirty minutes on Sunday, not only when you are sitting in church, not when you are trying to make a good impression.

Let it shine now ! That little word 'let' is the key to the whole issue. God will not force you. God's personality is contrary to human nature. He does not force a person to do anything. As I look back on my own life, I can honestly say to you that God never forced me to do one thing. Does that amaze you as much as it does me?

Permit me to explain. I can walk from behind the pulpit any time I desire and never return to a public platform again. I have the power and the will to say, "I'm tired. I have made my contribution to God and humanity. All that I have known since I was fourteen years of age is hard work. I have never used my life selfishly so far as I know, and now I feel that I owe some-thing to myself. I have made my final contribution to God and my fellow man. From here on out, I am going to take it easy !"

Of course, if I did that, I would be the most miserable person in the world. Even the very thought of it frightens me. But I use this example to point out that I have a will of my own whereby I can make up my mind to never preach another sermon. And God would never force me. He would never come down with a club and say, "Now look here, Kathryn. I force you to spend the rest of your life preaching the Gospel."

No, God will not force me to serve Him or to live a Christian life. I do it because I want to, because I love Him. My whole life revolves around a person and that person is Jesus Christ.

There is a place in Christ where one loves Him so much that he chooses to serve Him, that he wants to serve Him more than anything in the world. His vitality comes from God, his strength, his wisdom, his knowledge come from Him and his life is lived through and in Him because he is a part of the Body of Christ and wants to serve Him. Then it is the most natural thing in the world for that person to want to serve the brethren, and to serve all humanity. It is similar to the fact that 2+2=4.

God says, "Let your light shine." You have to WANT your light to shine. You are the master of your light. You may possess degrees in theology, you may be skilled and learned in the Word of God, you may have experienced the Baptism of the Holy Spirit and know the fullness of the Spirit; yet, you must LET the Holy Spirit work through you and shine His light through your life.

LET IT SHINE— always, everywhere. When you get out of bed each day you say joyously to yourself and to God, TO LIVE IS CHRIST. From that very moment, make up your mind to manifest something of the glory of Christ to everyone that you meet that day. Keep a watch over yourself. On many occasions, the garbage collectors have passed my kitchen door before I left the house for my office. It is my choice to either keep that door closed, pull down the shade and turn my back; or go to the door, greet them and wish them a good day, even though it was the noise of the garbage cans rattling throughout the neighboring community that awakened me before dawn and long before the truck reached my own driveway. God does not force me to make either of those two choices. I can be disgruntled and let my natural disposition take control of me, or I can choose to let my light shine. It's up to me!

Every morning when you awaken you make the choice. You can say, "For me to live is Christ" (Philippians 1:21), and Christ is love. You can manifest His glory and His love to the world and let your light shine for the Lord Jesus Christ. Or, you can decide to let your light be hid under the bushel, and go around grumpy, complaining, making yourself and everybody else miserable.

When you are an heir of God and a joint-heir with Christ Jesus, the whole person — body, soul and spirit — is affected. As I walk out on the street and during every moment of my life, I want my Lord to be proud of me, not only in soul and spirit, but of my outward appearance as well.

Let your loved ones in the home see your light and your victory. Let your fellow workers, whether you are in the office or the shop, in the factory or school, see that Christ is dwelling in your heart. Why shouldn't the tradesman, the postman, the bus driver perceive your secret? Be an open epistle of Christ known and read of all men everywhere, be a light whose brilliance cannot be dimmed.

The Secret

How is it that we all are so slow of heart to understand? Probably the best way to convey my case in point is to describe at some length the inner experiences of a man who had long been devoted to the service of God.

I am speaking of Hudson Taylor, a missionary to China. He left a letter written to his sister, a record of his search for holiness, for a deeper walk with God and the constant abiding in Christ Jesus. His letter reveals his total inability to find a means to obtain this deeper experience, despite the fact that the way lies clearly printed on the pages of scripture. Although this wonderful truth is indeed plainly outlined in God's Word, yet the Holy Spirit alone can make it a reality to the hearts of men and women. So, in this letter written to his sister, Hudson Taylor, that great missionary to China, expressed his deep emotions, his desperate search for this experience. I take the liberty to quote from this letter :

"'I prayed, fasted, agonized, made resolutions, read the Bible more diligently. sought more time for retirement and meditation ; but all without effect. Every day, almost every hour, the consciousness of sin oppressed me. Then came the question: "Is there no rescue? Must it be this to the end, constant conflict, and instead of victory, too often defeat?"

"I hated myself, I hated my sin, and yet I gained no strength against it. I felt I was a child of God, but how to rise to my privileges as a child I was utterly powerless to see. I thought that holiness, practical holiness, was to be gradually attained by a diligent use of the means of grace. I felt there was nothing I so much desired in the world, nothing I so much needed. When my agony of soul was at its height, a sentence in a letter was used to remove the scales from my eyes, and the Spirit of God revealed the truth of our oneness with Jesus."

Would you like to know ... to see what was in that letter, that one sentence that gave to Hudson Taylor that which he had sought so long? All right then — let's continue :

"By faith a channel is formed by which Christ's fullness plenteously flows down. The barren branch becomes a portion of the fruitful stem. He is most holy who has most of Christ within."

Let me repeat that one sentence. It is profound. If you forget everything else that this letter includes, if you do not read any farther, remember this one sentence : "He is most holy who has most of Christ within."

The letter continued, "It is defective faith that clogs the feet and causes many a fall. Abiding, not struggling or striving, looking to Him, trusting Him for present power, trusting Him to subdue all inward corruption, resting in the conscious joy of a complete salvation ; a salvation from all sin, willing that He should be truly supreme.

"That is not new, and yet," said Hudson Taylor, "it is new to me. I seem to have gotten to the edge only, but to the edge of a sea that is boundless. Not a striving to have faith, not a striving to increase our faith, not a struggle at all; but a looking to the Faithful One, looking to Jesus seems all we need — resting in the Lord, resting completely and entirely on Him for time and eternity."

That is the secret and that was the sentence which arrested Hudson Taylor's attention — that one sentence: "NOT A STRIVING TO HAVE FAITH, BUT A LOOKING OFF TO THE FAITHFUL ONE SEEMS ALL THAT WE NEED!" It's just that simple!

I shall never forget my conversion at the age of fourteen in that little Methodist Church in Concordia, Missouri, an experience I related earlier to you. It was some time after that that God so definitely called me to the ministry. My call to preach was as real as my conversion. It seemed that every atom of my being cried out for more of Jesus. I have known physical hunger but I have never known a physical hunger in my whole life that was as great as the spiritual hunger that I had for Him.

I was very ignorant and very stupid when it came to spiritual things. I had had no formal theological training, nothing whatsoever. But I stumbled upon some holiness camp meetings in Iowa after I became a Christian and before I knew anything about the Holy Spirit, before I learned about the Baptism with the Holy Spirit.

All I knew was that I had been born again, that Jesus had forgiven my sins. I shall always remember that old-fashioned tabernacle on the camp meeting grounds with sawdust underfoot. I was so hungry for more of Jesus and every time an altar call was given after the morning, the afternoon or night sessions, there I was, a red-headed, freckle-faced teen-aged girl rushing down the aisle, the first to kneel in that sawdust, my head buried in my arms, weeping and crying and seeking holiness, seeking some experience I knew not what.

When the noon hour came, everyone else would leave for dinner but I remained there at the altar. I would be there when the afternoon service began. I was the first to return to the altar when the call was given again for those who wanted to be completely holy, for those seeking holiness.

I never found what I was seeking THERE ! I was seeking for some experience, some ecstasy. It was years later that I learned that Jesus is our holiness, and the one who has the most of His holiness, is the one who has the most of Jesus. You may talk about the experience of holiness and sanctification. It is still a matter of seeking Jesus. You may talk about the wonderful experience of being filled with the Holy Spirit. It's still more of Jesus. And even after one has been filled with the Holy Spirit remember, my friend — the Holy Spirit Himself always magnifies and glorifies Jesus.

He is most holy who has most of Jesus within! No, it's not striving to have faith; it's not striving for some experience; but it's looking to Jesus, receiving more of Him, and that is your answer.

The Lord's Healing Touch
By Kathryn Kuhlman

Faith !

What a mighty word is faith.

What is it that rolls back the dark shadows of death to send the glorious light of the resurrection in all its brilliant beauty to the sorrowing heart? What is it that lifts the burdens that are too heavy to bear? What is it that brings cleansing to the sin-sick soul? What is it that cools the fevered brow, eases the torturing pain, and heals the afflicted and diseased?

The answer is FAITH.

But this is not faith for faith's sake, not a mere believing in something or someone. It is Holy Spirit imparted inspired faith. It is faith based on the teachings of the Word of God. It is faith, pure and simple, in the atoning merits of Jesus Christ who died on the cross for all men everywhere, and for you and me.

Faith is Christ-centered if it is Bible faith.

Someone has said : "Jesus will do everything for you that you really expect Him to do." Jesus meant something like that when He said, "According to your faith be it unto you." (Matthew 9:29)

There is a tragic dearth of faith today. Creeds, traditions, opinions : all these have somehow taken the place in the hearts of men (many professing to be Christians) of that kind of faith that moves mountains. Yet God is still in the heaven and stands ready to give a believing and living faith through Christ to anyone who will dare to receive.

In all probability, you feel the need of such a faith. That may well be the reason why you are reading this little book and why you are willing to meditate and pray about this most vital matter.

Your Faith

Even in the ranks of believers, there is as much confusion about what faith is, and what faith does, as about any other of the great themes of Christian thought.

Faith is the deed of trust.

Faith is belief in action.

Faith is the heart moving toward Jesus, receiving from Him.

Faith is the latchstring to God's great Supply House.

Faith is to be sought. It is not a matter of 'working up' faith. Faith does not come 'up' — it comes down! Faith is divine heart enrichment, the active moving of the Holy Spirit in believing exercise. Faith is from God, in Jesus' Name, anointed by the Third Person of the Trinity. One prays for faith. It is a gift from God.

In Mark, Chapter 5, Verses 25 through 34, we read

about a woman by the name of Lydia. She was in great need of the Lord as her physician, as many people are today — perhaps even you.

This young widow, once beautiful and vivacious, was wasted away, her attractiveness gone. She had a serious sick-ness peculiar to women. She had been treated by many physicians, but to no avail. They could do nothing for her and her illness persisted, worsening with each day. Great was her distress and she despaired of ever having a well and strong body again.

Then Jesus came! What mighty and miraculous changes are wrought when Jesus comes into homes, into lives and into hearts !

One day Lydia saw a multitude moving slowly past her home. Perhaps someone knocked on her door and told her that Jesus was in the midst of the crowd — that He could heal her. The very thought of being well must have made her heart fill with hope and joy. Oh, to be well and strong again, to be able to worship in the temple, to visit with friends !

But there were misgivings in Lydia's heart, too. From the vantage point of her home, she may have seen the nobleman, Jairus, earnestly in conversation with Jesus, for it was on that same day that this nobleman had come to Capernaum to ask Jesus to come to the bedside of his sick young daughter. Would Jesus have time for her, too?

Besides, there were so many people around Jesus. They had come from far and wide from other communities to see and hear the Miracle Worker and Teacher, and Lydia knew it would be difficult to press her way to Jesus through the throng.

Lydia, however, was desperate. She put all her fears aside. She made her decision and acted upon it, and hurried to the street as fast as her weakened condition permitted and, timidly at first, began to elbow her way through the crowds. A few stragglers permitted her to go by them but soon she was thrust against a mass of humanity such as she had never experienced before, and she could go no farther.

What shall I do? Where will I go? were questions she must have asked herself. She dropped to her knees. She was so weak, and it seemed hopeless that she could reach Jesus. Suddenly she saw an opening before her, and still on her knees, she began to crawl carefully but determinedly. Many a dirty sandal must have pressed down on her thin hands, but finally, nearing exhaustion, she reached the inner circle of the crowd. She lifted her dust covered face, and there He was — Jesus.

If only she could attract His attention, if only she could cry out, but He was speaking. Within her reach, however, was the hem of His garment, the wide band that encircled His robe. She was a Jewess and was well acquainted with the meaning of that border, that God had commanded His people to wear that band as evidence they were keeping His law. To Lydia, the border represented even more : Jesus' deity, the profession of who and what He was. She believed that Jesus was all He claimed to be. This was her faith.

Lydia balanced herself in her crouched position and exerting all the strength she had, she reached out, her fingers reverently touching the hem of Jesus' garment while saying in her heart, "If I can but touch His garment, I shall be whole."

Immediately she was healed and at the same moment, Jesus knew that someone had touched Him

— in faith. There was a vast difference between that touch of faith and the press of the curious who gathered around Jesus. He knew Lydia's faith had touched Him — she knew she was whole again.

A Reasonable Doctrine

The New Testament records many miracles of healing such as took place in Capernaum that day. But you may be asking the question, Can and will Jesus perform miracles of healing today? Did such miracles cease with the closing of Christ's earthly ministry?

These are reasonable questions worthy of reasonable answers. Surely there is more involved than the mere statement of an historical fact in the assertion that "he cast out the spirits with his word, and healed all that were sick." (Matthew 8:16)

There is no "day of miracles"! Miracles are the manifestation of the power of God. This marvelous power was manifested throughout the dispensation of God the Father, throughout the dispensation of Jesus Christ the Son, and continues to be manifested during this dispensation of the Holy Spirit. Whenever God works, it is in a supernatural way; therefore, miracles will continue as long as God is still on His throne. Let me repeat: there is no "day of miracles" with God!

While it is certainly true that faith is more a matter of the heart than it is of the head, this in no way excludes the utter reasonableness of the doctrine which is often referred to as "divine healing." This term, if used in the sense of Christ's healing power, means that one is healed in answer to the prayer of faith in the name of Jesus as God's Son, the sacrifice on Calvary. For this healing power. He and He alone should receive glory and praise.

This doctrine (truth) is a most rational one, and may well be received as such by everyone who believes on Jesus as Savior. It is not difficult to understand, and less difficult to believe.

It is fact that many Christians have far more potential faith than they realize. To illustrate : do you believe that God the Father is the only true and living God? Do you accept the truth that Jesus Christ is God's Son, born of a virgin, crucified, dead, buried, raised from the dead? If you can honestly answer "yes" to these questions, you have good foundation for miracle-provoking faith, and if this potential faith is given free course, allowed to act and become deed, you will experience answered prayer.

Kathryn Kuhlman

What all this means is simply that you have already laid the groundwork within your heart for the performance of the miracle of healing. Take encouragement from this fact. Press through your pride, through your unbelief, your pre-conceived opinions. Press through on your knees and exercise your belief in the Great Physician who will make you every whit whole. Look up and praise God — worship Him — adore Jesus — let your heart rise above the discord of the world around you and praise God for all He has done for you, and what He is going to do!

Go a little further and let your heart and mind fasten on the knowledge that you can KNOW that you are going to be healed. It is reasonable to expect it because at the heart of your faith stands a person, Jesus Christ, the Eternal Son. The only thing in existence that can limit His power is your unbelief.

Sickness is Christ's enemy. If sin had not come into the world, there would be no sickness; and when we are with Christ in glory, there will be no pain and no affliction. These came into the world as a direct result

OBJECT OF FAITH IS A PERSON — THE BIBLE WORD(S) ARE THE FINGERS of sin. But remember that many are sick or afflicted through no act of sin on their part, and we must never stand in judgment, pointing our linger at one who is sick, and declare that their sickness is because of sin in their life.

You may not be familiar with the expression, "slain by the Spirit," a terminology used when one receives a tremendous outpouring of the blessing of God; but this is simply a "foretaste of glory divine," an earnest of glorious resurrection power that we shall all experience when this mortal body puts on immortality. Through the price that Christ paid on Calvary, we may all have "an earnest of our inheritance," the "life also of Jesus — made manifest in our mortal flesh," until our work here on earth is finished. Because our eternal destiny concerns both spirit and body, our redemption also must be spiritual and physical. We cannot receive our full inheritance until the coming Day of Redemption, but we can enjoy the "earnest of our redemption" now. In the very same way that we experience the first fruits of our spiritual salvation, we can also receive the first fruits of our physical salvation : healing for the body.

Remember, our bodies are the temples of the Holy Spirit and the Holy Spirit is a quickening, life-giving power. Paul wrote to the church at Rome in these words: "But if the Spirit of him (the Holy Spirit) that raised up Jesus from the dead dwell in you, he that raised up Christ from the dead shall also quicken your mortal (flesh and blood) bodies by his Spirit that dwelleth in you." (Romans 8:11)

The question may now justifiably arise as to whom this can be applied. Who has the right, according to the scriptures, to expect the Holy Spirit — this quickening power of God — to be exerted in his behalf in the healing of his body? Do you have such a right? Isn't that what you would like to know?

Turn to Romans, Chapter 8, Verse 9: "But ye are not in the flesh, but in the Spirit, if so be that the Spirit of God (the Holy Spirit) dwell in you. Now if any man have not the Spirit of Christ (the Holy Spirit), he is none of his."

What Paul is saying is that every true born-again believer has the Holy Spirit dwelling within him. He may not have the Holy Spirit in His fullness, but he does have the witnessing presence of the Holy Spirit, else there is no assurance that he is saved. So, in this plain light, it can be seen that every Christian has the right to look to Jesus Christ for the healing of his body.

To pray for healing with the faith destroying words, "if it be Thy Will," is like trying to grow corn without planting seed. Imagine a man standing before his garden and praying, "Lord, give me corn in my garden, if it be Thy Will." He returns six weeks later and there is no corn. He accepts as fact it was not God's Will that he should grow corn, when the real fact is that his field produced no corn because he planted no seed!

God calls His words, which are spirit and life, "seed." Corn planted in the ground produces corn, and the Word of God (His "seed") planted in hearts produces the result which the Word of God promises. It is impossible to believe God for healing until you are convinced beyond a shadow of doubt that it is His will to heal your body.

The same Lord who "wills" your salvation ("The

Lord is not willing that any should perish" II Peter 3:9), also "wills" your healing ("Himself took our infirmities, and bare our sicknesses" Matthew 8:17). Physical healing is as much a part of the atonement as is salvation for the soul.

The Psalmist in an ecstasy of praise exclaimed : "Bless the Lord, my soul, and forget not all his benefits. Who forgiveth all thine iniquities; who healeth all thy diseases." (Psalm 103:2, 3)

There go all our sins and our sicknesses !

Looking down through the telescope of time, the prophet Isaiah saw Christ hanging on the cross and declared : "He (Jesus) was wounded for our transgressions, he was bruised for our iniquities . . . and with his stripes we are healed." (Isaiah 53:5) Isaiah's prophecy is confirmed in the New Testament: "When Jesus was come into Peter's house, he saw his wife's mother laid, and sick of a fever. And he touched her hand, and the fever left her: and she arose, and ministered unto them . . . and he healed all that were sick : that it might be fulfilled which was spoken by

Esaias the prophet, saying. Himself took our infirmities, and bare our sicknesses," (Matthew 8:14-17) This is the "double cure" for soul and body !

The scriptures constantly confront us with the wholesomeness of Jesus. In His earthly ministry, He was often challenged by pain, sickness and disease in every conceivable form : blindness, lameness, leprosy. In no case did Jesus register a negative heart. In every case He was "moved with compassion." It was His very nature, His characteristic, to be moved with non-resistant compassion whenever and wherever He came face to face with a human need. In every situation He did something about it. In every instance He gloriously and victoriously met that need. Jesus still moves with compassion today. "Jesus Christ the same yesterday, and today, and forever." (Hebrews 13:8)

God's mighty power has never changed! Does Jesus still possess the power to work miracles, forgive sins, lift burdens, heal bodies? Surely He would have left some pronouncement before He went away to Glory — or He would have immediately sent an inspired messenger to tell us, if He no longer could do these mighty things for us.

He gave us His Word: "All power is given unto me in heaven and in earth," and He spoke this in connection with the great commission : "Go ye therefore, and teach all nations, baptizing them in the name of the Father, and of the Son, and of the Holy Ghost : teaching them to observe all things whatsoever I have commanded you : and, lo, I am with you always, even unto the end of the world." (Matthew 28:18-20)

Far from suggesting a lessening of His power, Jesus magnified His continued and enlarged capacity to exercise it. Here He spoke plainly and concisely of the time AFTER His ascension when He would take His place at the Father's right hand : "And these signs shall follow them that believe; In my name shall they cast out devils . . . THEY SHALL LAY HANDS ON THE SICK, AND THEY SHALL RECOVER" (Mark 16:17-20). After saying this, He was taken up in the clouds. Therefore, it is evident to all that the last word from Christ was to expect the further demonstration of His power in all phases of the gospel ministry : salvation for the soul and healing for the body. Physical healing was not unknown to Old Testament saints and while there are many instances, let us recount just a few here :

"And God said, If thou wilt diligently hearken to the voice of the Lord thy God . . . and keep all his statutes, I will put none of these diseases upon thee, which I have brought upon the Egyptians : for I am the Lord that healeth thee." (Exodus 15:26) Of a certainty, God was speaking of PHYSICAL, not spiritual healing.

Read in your Bible Isaiah 53 :4, 5 : "He was wounded for our transgressions, he was bruised for our iniquities: the chastisement of our peace was upon him ; and with his stripes we are healed." In these glowing verses is the gospel as revealed throughout the entire Word of God: salvation for the soul and healing for the body.

Miracles of Healing

It is strangely apparent that many of God's own people shy away from any discussion of the miracle-working power of Christ; that is, from any discussion of that power in present day exercise. For the most part, they are willing to permit the record of the supernatural performances of the long ago days to stand ; but they seem extremely hesitant to voice testimony that they have faith in Him for these mighty works in this modern day.

It would seem that every child of God would meet the issue with joy in view of the needs in every life ; or, that they would cherish an opportunity to bring glory to the One who died for their redemption.

How great a change would be effected in the church ; what a challenge would be laid at the door of the unbeliever, if God's people dared to make trust a deed, and to exercise belief in faith !

Those who know me are aware of my great respect for doctors and their vast medical and scientific knowledge; and without any desire or thought to belittle their sincere efforts, let it be said that God can and will do what no man can do in healing ALL who will come to Him by faith in the name of His Son. He is no respecter of persons.

The power of God will become real to your heart in a beautiful way when He touches your body and the healing virtue of Jesus Christ flows through you. It will enhance the spiritual blessings which you may have enjoyed for a long time. It will enrich your testimony. It will enable you to encourage others who stand in great need. It will challenge the unsaved, and may well be the means of leading others to a saving knowledge of the Lord Jesus Christ, by far the greatest miracle of all.

Since God, His Son Jesus and the Holy Spirit are supernatural, it is natural that we should expect God to do supernatural things for us. We can live in the state of expectancy that He will perform miracles and among them are miracles of healing for our physical bodies, healing all who will reach out and touch the hem of His garment, all who will say, "Jesus, You are all You claim to be."

The place that the Word of God needs to occupy

has been yielded to tradition. Doubt has robbed many of us of the re-wards that result when we believe God's promises. Opinions have usurped the seat of God's positive declarations. God's people have become eloquent in excuses allowing an almost total lack of evidence of a living Christ in their lives. Jesus is as willing to heal today as He was when a leper cried out to Him : "Lord, if thou wilt, thou canst make me clean. And Jesus put forth his hand and touched him, saying, I will : be thou clean. And immediately his leprosy was cleansed." (Matthew 8:2, 3)

The Healing Virtue

The healing virtue, or power, that Jesus uses is the Holy Spirit, the Third Person of the Godhead. To understand something of His personality and His work will make it easier for you to bring belief to the stature of faith.

Let this simple statement sink into the very deepest recesses of your heart. The Holy Spirit can and will do anything and everything for you that Jesus Himself would do. He standing there before you with His hands extended and the radiant light of glory shining from His face. In fact, Jesus sent the Holy Spirit when He went to be with the Father : "I will pray the Father, and he shall give you another Comforter, that he may abide with you forever."

That glorious promise in John 14:16 says several startling things. It shows the three members of the Godhead in divine harmony of action. It reveals that the Holy Spirit will be "another" like unto Himself, a Comforter, a Strengthener. It shows that the Holy Spirit will continue and abide "forever."

Instead of the Great Physician having limitations of the flesh, accessible to a relatively small number, He becomes accessible to ALL of us through the Holy Spirit. The Great Physician is everywhere today. He is all-sufficient for Jesus not only has power in heaven, but all power in earth as well.

This fact alone should be enough to change our entire outlook. It is not merely a matter of getting something from God, as important as that may be to you. It is a matter of "practicing the presence of God," of recognizing, enjoying and utilizing the continual abiding presence of the Holy Spirit.

Remember that the Holy Spirit is with you whether you think so or not, whether you feel His presence or are wholly unaware of it. If you are a true child of God, then you have the witness of the Holy Spirit which is your assurance of salvation. This Holy Spirit is the same One who worked with Jesus during His earthly ministry in the performance of His healing miracles.

To understand that enables you to see what great power there is available to you now. It is the same as when Jesus walked the shores of Galilee. The only difference is that you have MORE on which to base your faith, for His testimony has been established and corroborated thousands of times and more since then.

When Lydia touched the hem of the Lord's garment, the Word declares : "And Jesus, immediately knowing in himself that virtue had gone out of him, turned about in the press, and said. Who touched my clothes?"

The virtue that "had gone out of him" was the power of the Holy Spirit flowing through His very being. It did not mean that He had any the less of that power because He had been touched by Lydia, but that another through Him had received of it.

One ordinarily thinks of virtue as being a "specific kind of goodness" or characteristic. That is true. The kind of goodness in this instance is the divine nature, the perfection, the holiness and righteousness of Almighty God. This is one point on which many fail in their understanding of how God works in the healing of the body, or in answering prayer for any benefit or blessing. They fail to see that they are asking God to touch them with the high zenith of absolute purity, the power of perfect holiness. That is His virtue.

We should realize, therefore, that this requires prayerful consideration; that sincere, earnest, honest heart cleansing should precede any request of the Lord to exercise this virtue for our benefit. Far better that we come to Him pleading His mercy, "Lord, cleanse my heart with the precious blood of the Lamb. Make me pure and clean from all my sin. Make my heart right in the sight of God," than to come with the attitude that He must heal us in spite of the sinful condition of our lives, or without any desire on our part to serve Him, or to render Him glory in testimony after He does heal us. Remember, you ask for a part of God when you ask Him to give of His virtue and His power.

In other words, remember to come unto the Lord with all the heart warmth and utter reverence that you would feel if you were to suddenly find yourself confronted by the Person of the Son of God, for the Holy Spirit is God in exactly the same way as Jesus is God, and as the Father is God.

Jesus Christ now sits at the right hand of God the Father in glory. He still has the body of Calvary and bears the scars of the crucifixion. He is our Savior, and

He is in position of great High Priest.

The Holy Spirit is here. He is with us now. We can feel His presence, practice His presence, utilize His presence, praise God in His presence and live under the blood of Jesus in His presence. Let it be said that this healing virtue is obtained through Christ and in no other way. All that is done by the Holy Spirit is done in the name of Jesus, and the Holy Spirit will definitely lead you to give Jesus all the glory for your healing after He has touched you. The Holy Spirit is carrying out the injunction of Jesus when He is with you, when He blesses you, when He keeps you, when He heals you. Remember that Jesus sent the Holy Spirit when He returned to the Father in Heaven.

Lest someone feel that the work of healing sick bodies is given precedence over the greater ministry of the Holy Spirit in bringing conviction and conversion to the unsaved, it must be pointed out in this connection that the same power that heals sick bodies also convicts and saves. There is but one Holy Spirit and whenever and wherever He is present for healing the sick, He is also present in revival power. In fact, many great revivals have resulted from the performance of healing miracles. That was true in the

Lord's ministry to such an extent that He even told that He was healing so that they might believe also for salvation.

Church members today need to stop limiting the ministry of the Holy Spirit, and begin praying and believing God for the enriching and enlarging work of the Third Person of the Trinity in His blessed fullness. Jesus meant the Holy Spirit to be as Himself among us until the very end of this age, which will close when He returns at the Catching Up. The 'touch of the Lord' is the moving of the Holy Spirit in us, through us, and for us. He will supply any and every need in your life when you will simply believe God.

How To Touch the Lord

In Mark's account of the healing of Lydia, she is referred to as a "certain woman," and so also are you a certain man or a certain woman in the sight of the Lord today. It is as though you are the only person in all the world in need of His touch, and though you may be in a vast multitude, God will single you out if you touch Him by faith.

Matthew records that Lydia "said within herself, If I may but touch his garment, I shall be whole." Her discussion and persuasion were within her own heart. She knew in herself that Jesus would heal her, and so she was healed. This is how to "touch" the Lord: be absolutely persuaded in your own heart that He will meet your need.

Lydia had an urgent need of the Lord's help. That need was so great that all lesser things were relegated to lesser places of importance in her consideration. Her consuming thought was for the healing of her body. She was desperate about the matter. She did not approach the Lord with the idea that IF He healed her, it would be wonderful; and that IF He did not heal her, she would not be too much surprised or disappointed. Her need was far too great for that. She already knew that medically speaking, there was no help. She went to Jesus with her whole heart and mind as well as with her sick body. That is how to touch the Lord: with a whole heart and a mind single to His performing the need of the hour.

Lydia had no other hope. It was Jesus and Jesus only who held the answer to her dilemma, and those of us who reach that place in the concentration of our need and our faith, will surely know the Lord's healing touch.

Sometimes it is not easy to reach the Lord, for there are obstacles such as Lydia knew. There was her weakness to be considered. Her strength and her life's blood were far spent. Besides, hundreds of people were milling about Jesus, each seeking for himself a better view, a clearer hearing, or a gratification of his own curiosity or heart hunger. People often stand in the way when one is trying to get closer to Jesus, close enough to reach out and touch Him. Most often they are well meaning people, but we fear what they will think or what they will say. Instead, we need to be encouraged to trust the Lord, and this assurance is many times found on our knees in prayer.

Press through, beloved, press through ! No matter who may stand in the way, press through. You need not explain or make your determination audible, just simply and persistently press through to Jesus. Lydia made a desperate effort to reach her Lord, and He was there to honor her faith and to meet her need. She merely touched the hem of the Master's robe. She did not handle Him, she did not tug at Him, she touched His garment, but that was enough. This started the mighty power of the Holy Spirit coursing through her body and made her well and whole again. No, Lydia was not worthy to touch Jesus (and neither are we) ; yet, she knew that He forgave sins when He healed, and that He healed all manner of sickness and disease. She knew He had never turned anyone away who came to Him, and she knew to reverence Him as the Holy One, the Son of the Living God.

The Prayer of Faith

The true prayer of faith may be just that and nothing more. It would seem from the record that Jairus' word to Jesus was that kind of prayer: "My little daughter lieth at the point of death : I pray thee, come and lay thy hands on her, that she may be healed; and she shall live." Of course Jesus went and even though the little child had died before He reached her bedside, she was raised up by the power of God. No matter what the need, Jairus saw Jesus ready, willing and able to heal.

The prayer of faith is in reality the heart act of receiving that which we ask the Lord to do. "Now, faith is the substance of things hoped for ... " (Hebrews 11:1) "Believe that ye receive it." (Mark 11:24) It is not the mere act of petitioning the Lord and certainly not the condition of begging. It is the heart act of receiving from the Lord with the positive knowledge that the material evidences are to be made known at His pleasure, for your good, and for His glory.

Perhaps you are saying at this point, "I would give anything in the world for a faith like that;" but do not start trying to measure your faith to see how great or how small it is. By the time you are finished, you may likely seem to have no faith at all. Don't try to "take your faith out" and look at it. Your faith is the result, at any given time, of your heart relation to Jesus. Surely you have experienced moments when you have exercised great faith, and other times when you feel your faith is small. Begin your season of petitioning with consecration, with praise, with worship, "be careful for nothing; but in everything by prayer and supplication with THANKSGIVING let your requests be made known unto God." (Philippians 4:6)

The prayer of faith is not the result of having used a measuring rod to find a level on your state of belief at a given moment. Neither is the fact that at one time you received a mighty answer to prayer, definite proof that you have faith now; nor the fact that you never had an acknowledged answer to prayer, any reason to believe that you cannot pray the prayer of faith today.

Your faith is the result of your heart relation to Jesus. Surely there are times when you will exercise great faith and other times when you feel that you have little faith. This is why the prescribed formula begins with praise, worship, consecration, thankfulness for past favors and blessings. This is why faith is great when a spiritual revival is in progress ; why God's child, awed by the beauty of Jesus, the surety of the Word, the goodness of the Father and the sweet presence of the Spirit, can easily believe for anything and everything.

The prayer of faith, then, should be the experience of every believer, enriching his testimony, making joyous his heart, and a source of praise to Him who hears and answers prayer.

Foundation of Faith

That great prince among preachers, Charles Spurgeon, is often quoted as saying, concerning praying the prayer of faith: "Plead a promise." His advice has been proven sound and good — it works !

The Bible is God's Word and is the foundation for faith. God said what He meant, and meant what He said ; and it is true that there is a promise in the Bible to meet every need. There are many blessed promises on which to stand for the healing of the body.

Concerning the record of miracles performed by Jesus in His earthly ministry, Matthew gives as Christ's reason for doing these works : 'That it might be fulfilled which was spoken by Esaias the prophet, saying, Himself took our infirmities, and bare our sicknesses." (Matthew 8:17) Rejoice and praise His Holy Name because He bore your infirmities and sicknesses as surely as He bore the diseases of those whom He healed near Peter's home that afternoon, and all the others who came to know the healing touch of Jesus.

Consider the statement, clear and bold, in I Peter 2:24: "Who (Jesus) his own self bare our sins in his own body on the tree, that we, being dead to sins, should live unto righteousness : by whose stripes we are healed." By whose stripes YOU are healed. Is that not sufficient foundation for your faith?

In the Epistle of James we find many thoroughly practical and workable statements that are especially pointed toward the church at large, and in a very definite way for the entire church age. One such passage is found in James 5:7-16:

"Be patient therefore, brethren, unto the coming of the Lord. Behold, the husbandman waiteth for the precious fruit of the earth, and hath long patience for it, until he receive the early and latter rain.

"Be ye also patient; establish your hearts : for the coming of the Lord draweth nigh.

"Grudge not one against another, brethren, lest ye be condemned : behold, the judge standeth before the door.

"Take, my brethren, the prophets, who have spoken in the name of the Lord, for an example of suffering affliction, and of patience.

"Behold, we count them happy which endure. Ye have heard of the patience of Job, and have seen the end of the Lord : that the Lord is very pitiful, and of tender mercy.

"But above all things, my brethren, swear not, neither by heaven, neither by the earth, neither by any other oath : but let your yea be yea; and your nay, nay; lest ye fall into condemnation.

"Is any among you afflicted? let him pray. Is any merry? let him sing psalms.

"Is any sick among you? let him call for the elders of the church ; and let them pray over him, anointing him with oil in the name of the Lord :

"And the prayer of faith shall save the sick, and the Lord shall raise him up ; and if he have committed sins, they shall be forgiven him.

"Confess your faults one to another, and pray one for another, that ye may be healed. The effectual fervent prayer of a righteous man availeth much."

Wrapped up together in such a short passage of scripture are enough Holy Spirit inspired statements that an entire revival campaign might well be based on them alone. If God's people will fulfill the injunctions of these verses, the lost will come with broken hearts, crying to be shown the way to a salvation like this.

Consider briefly what we have read in this Epistle of James : An admonition to abide patiently until the return of Jesus for the church with the promise that His coming "draweth nigh;" an urgent appeal for the manifestation of the spirit of brotherly love among believers ; a challenge to exampleship under persecution ; an exhortation against swearing ; and a "prescription" for the sick in the ranks of believers during the church age.

This last we will examine carefully in the light of the knowledge that it is meant for us now — today. That is a foundation for our faith.

"Is any among you afflicted? ... is any merry? ... is any sick among you?" There is fulfillment of every need in the Lord's great program, all the way from giving vent to the heart-bursting and overflowing joy of the supernal blessings of salvation, to the lifting of affliction and the healing of sicknesses. Whatever is the need, Jesus meets that need.

The Bible Prescription

Giving rightful credence to the intent of the Word in the passage quoted earlier in James, let us examine the "prescription" given for the sick and afflicted among the ranks of believers:

"Let him pray." This presents the thought that the needy one is going to ascertain his present relationship with his Lord. If there is something in his heart that might prevent the Lord from healing him, the Holy Spirit has the opportunity to convict him of that fact and lead him to repentance, thus permitting him to make the next step with the assurance that there is nothing between his soul and the Savior.

In prayer, the believer has the further opportunity to deepen his consecration, and to progress in his experience in the Holy Spirit. His heart will come under the anointing of the Holy Spirit for the praise and adoration that will cause him to lean heavily on the Lord for his healing.

The believer will renew his covenants with the Lord. He will make a new covenant, vowing to be more energetic in his service to God after receiving his healing. He will be more faithful in discharging his obligations to the Lord and His work at large.

Thus, in his season of prayer, the believer will find his heart prepared for the other phases of the healing "prescription" recorded by James.

"Let him call for the elders of the church." Those ministers of the gospel who may be known to the believer, or in whose ministry he has found especial blessing, will be called to him, if he is unable to go to the place of worship. They will join together, and with him, pray and believe God in the name of Jesus to heal him. In connection with this season of prayer, the elders are to anoint the believer with oil in the name of the Lord.

Anointing With Oil

There is blessed significance in the use of oil (olive oil) in the scriptures. The holy things of the tabernacle were anointed with oil to signify a separation for God's use and service, as in Exodus 30:25. It was used to signify a place of special blessing as when Jacob anointed the stones after the divine revelation in his dream, recorded in Genesis 28. That which was anointed was to become the object of divine protection, as in Psalm 105:15: 'Touch not mine anointed." Oil was used as a type of great spiritual blessing: "Thou anointest my head with oil." (Psalm 23:5)

It is not strange, therefore, that oil is used by James as a type of the Holy Spirit in the "prescription." The Holy Spirit was evidenced in the initial creation ; the Spirit of the Lord rested upon the prophets of old ; Jesus was conceived by the Holy Ghost ; He was the virtue of Christ's miracles in His earthly ministry; it is the unpardonable sin to blaspheme Him; and it is the Holy Spirit who will lift the believers in the rapture when Jesus comes again.

Do we not see, then, something of the meaning of the anointing oil as used by James? It is the calling and the recognition of the Holy Spirit in action. It is the testimony in connection with the healing of the sick and the afflicted that God alone is given the glory for the miracle wrought in answer to the prayer of faith.

It is not an over-statement to say that this is one of the sacred ordinances of the Church of Jesus Christ. The pitiable and tragic fact that it is neglected, or disbelieved, does not in the least alter its provisions, and its Bible-founded factuality. It is a privilege, through Calvary, because it is by "His stripes we are healed." There are many, a great many, today who have believed these words and have been blessedly healed.

The Healing Testimony

In a large measure, God's plan for the dissemination of the gospel message since the founding of the church has been the ministry of the testimony. It seems that God has ordained that word of mouth, the printed page, and any other means at hand, should be used to tell men what the Lord has done. Most of us have been saved because of the prayers and testimonies of others. What is true in the matter of soul winning, is also true with regard to the healing testimony; others are led to a sharing of the blessing.

There is a real "art" in giving a testimony. Perhaps the easiest way of all is to stand in a group of sympathetic and interested believers and tell how the Lord answered prayer for the healing of the body.

While it is imperative that we tell it far and wide that Jesus still saves through the blood, and that He still heals sick bodies and performs miracles in answer to the prayer of faith, we must be constantly in prayer for two things : pray that God will send the "seasons" of testimony, and then that He will give us the special anointing" that we need to take full and rich advantage of all the opportunities the Holy Spirit opens to us. In that way, the matter of testifying becomes a true partnership between the believer and the Holy Spirit. That is the unbeatable combination for soul winning and faith ministry.

Let it be stressed emphatically that we are not to hide the light of our testimony under the "bushel." The story must be told, and there have been many who did not keep their healing because they did not keep their covenant with the Lord in their testimony.

Perhaps, too, it will be well to state in this connection that a dogmatic attitude defeats the purpose of the testimony. Any effort to make a poor sick man feel that he is committing a terrible sin because he has a doctor or takes medication is nothing short of fanaticism. A sick man needs help, not condemnation. His heart needs to be made tender, and not rebellious. He needs to know that there is healing for him in Jesus' name, not to be made to feel like a sinner because he didn't know how to believe God.

There are many fine doctors, and they have done, and are doing, great humanitarian work in the world. They are doing much to alleviate suffering and it would be a falsehood to say that they are not instruments in God's hands and vitally needed. Many are alive today because of the kindly, sincere and intelligent care given by a good doctor or nurse. The Christian believer should be the first to recognize and appreciate this fact. What a tragedy it would be if there were no doctors, no hospitals, no medical skills to aid the suffering of mankind.

But there is another way, a way for one who will put his whole trust in Jesus : the miraculous way. There is a way when men have done all they can and the afflicted one turns to Jesus in desperation as Lydia did. He heals all who come to Him by faith.

Just remember, when the Lord has healed you, be

a faithful steward of your testimony. Take advantage of your special knowledge from experience of the Master's touch. Tell it, tell it to the great and small, tell it wherever you go. One day you may come to realize that the best part of your healing — as your salvation — is the privilege of using your blessings to reach the hearts of others with His Word.

Kathryn Kuhlman

Conclusion

In closing, let me say that this is not an effort to make an issue of divine healing. The issue is faith in God, whether or not we take Him at His Word.

From today on, keep so close to Jesus in Bible reading, in prayer, in testimony and in the fellowship of believers that faith becomes the order of your every day. What may now seem beyond the realm of plausibility, or even possibility, can become the general state of heart expectancy. You will no longer be surprised to see God do great and wonderful things in answer to prayer; but rather, you will be bitterly disappointed if the time comes when you do not expect Him to do mighty things.

Having known the Lord's healing touch, you can never be quite the same again. While His Spirit was effecting a change in your physical condition, you will find that He was also doing something to your heart. You have become the steward of another great

blessing. You have been given another link of

kinship with the blessed saints of long ago, who learned to trust God with every care. You have been given another assurance that Jesus lives, that He does have "all power."

In following Jesus and in growing in His grace, within your heart will re-echo words something like those Lydia heard : "Daughter, thy faith hath made thee whole; go in peace, and be whole of thy plague."

(Editor's Note: Years after Kathryn Kuhlman wrote the preceding chapters, God gave her an understanding of yet greater spiritual depths and a realization of the vast mercy and love of God transcending all human comprehension. His compassion knows no bounds or limits — His desire to reach hearts of men and women goes BEYOND the scope of His promises, beyond the prescribed methods of healing. For this reason, we are taking the liberty to quote from a later book by Kathryn Kuhlman, "God Can Do It Again," written in 1969.)

It is because of God's great love, compassion and mercy, that He gives anything to us. Often we lose sight of the fact that not one of us can claim any righteousness of our own, not one is worthy of the smallest blessing, but we are the receivers of His blessing because of His mercy and compassion. Healing is the sovereign act of God.

When I was very young, I could have given you all the answers. My theology was straight and I was sure that if you followed certain rules, worked hard enough, obeyed all the commandments, and had yourself in a certain spiritual state, God would heal you.

Lo and behold, my theology came tumbling down and was crushed into a thousand pieces when one day a man who had just entered the auditorium during a miracle service stood silently against the back wall, and after not more than five minutes, walked boldly to the stage and freely admitted, "My ear has just opened and I do not believe!'

Although I questioned him repeatedly, he never recanted. Seeing the crowd, out of curiosity, he came in not knowing whether it was an auction or some kind of giveaway program. He was standing there as a spectator and after much questioning, I found out that he had not been to church for more than twenty-five years and had put himself in the category of an atheist. It is possible for me to relate many cases where people have been healed who were amazed, who freely admitted that they did not expect to be healed, who sobbingly cried, "I cannot believe it — I cannot believe it." Until we have a way of defining it, all that I can tell you is that these are mercy healings. They have been healed through the mercy of the Lord.

We forget the mercy of God — we forget His great compassion — we forget that we do not earn our blessings ; neither do we merit His goodness. Were it not for the mercy and the compassion and the grace and the love of God, not one of us would be a Christian and the same holds true when it comes to physical healing. How often I have thought that God cares very little about man's theology, and we are so prone to get dogmatic about things that we know so little about !

There are some things in life which will always be unanswerable because we see through a glass darkly. God knows the beginning to the end, while all we can do is catch a glimpse of the present, and a distorted glimpse at that.

In 1865, when President Lincoln was assassinated — the great, patient, mighty Lincoln — an excited throng of thousands gathered in the streets of Washington, They were utterly bewildered, going to and fro as sheep without any shepherd. They were overcome by questions and emotions incident to that tragic hour. But in the midst of the tragic turmoil a man appeared on the steps of the Capitol and said, "God reigns and the government at Washington still lives." The crowds dispersed quietly. The right words had been said : "GOD REIGNS!"

Kathryn Kuhlman

A Message to the readers of this book :

Many of the radio messages by Kathryn Kuhlman are still available on cassette tape. If you desire any of her talks, you may request a listing of subjects by writing to :

The Kathryn Kuhlman Foundation

Post Office Box 3

Pittsburgh, PA 15230

Made in the USA
San Bernardino, CA
03 December 2019